Cryptocurrencies and Blockchain 2022

Cryptocurrencies and the blockchain are the future of your investments

I0037114

Contents

Introduction

Cryptocurrency, and the blockchain technology that makes it possible, is a societal revolution nothing short of Henry Ford's automobile, the printing press, or the Internet itself. In slightly more than a decade, cryptocurrency has rewritten a lot of the ways that both business and finance happen, and are seen as a tremendous element of change to some, and as a threat to others. Like other forms of digital technology, there can be a barrier to understanding the science, the process, and the benefits of cryptocurrency because it has no physical representation. Everyone has heard about Bitcoin, but no one has ever held one in their hands, nor will they. When used correctly, blockchain technology is more secure than the vault at Fort Knox, but there is no way to go on a tour of it. The purpose of this text is to give you a brief history of both technologies, where they began, how they have evolved, what they are being used for today and where they are headed in the future. Whether you are cryptocurrency's biggest fan or biggest skeptic, it is our hope that you come out of this book with more knowledge, more history, and the ability to make your own decision on what role cryptocurrency and blockchain will play in your future.

Chapter 1
Defining Cryptocurrency

To define cryptocurrency, we must break it into the two words it originates from. "Currency" is an easy enough one to digest, we all have known about currency for our entire lives. It is the representation of value we set on things and use to buy and sell items. Currencies are different all around the world, but as the world becomes smaller and more digitized, they are quickly becoming similar as more and more transactions are done online without the exchange of any sort of hard currency. For instance, say an American art collector has his eye on a rare painting being sold at Christie's London auction house. He does not have to attend the auction online in the 21st century, he can merely log on and bid remotely. The price of the painting will be in British pound sterling, but the American collector does not have to go to the local exchange and convert his dollars. He merely places his bids online knowing that there is a mechanism on his dashboard converting the dollar amounts back and forth from dollars to pounds. When he secures the painting, he confirms the dollar amount, his bank sends it along to Christie's account where it appears as pounds in the auction house bank account. He never sees the pound sterling and Christie's never see the dollars; it is a completely digital process.

While 'blockchain', 'cryptocurrency,' and 'bitcoin' are all terms that frequently get tied together, there's a major difference between them.

Bitcoin is a type of cryptocurrency. Blockchain stands alone as a type of technology that, while used by crypto, has seemingly limitless applications across a wide spectrum of industries.

At its core, blockchain is a ledger that records a history of transactions. It is transparent to all users and it cannot be altered.

If you're more familiar with the world where everything was done on paper and filed away in a cabinet somewhere, envision it as the world's greatest paper trail in that everyone can access the original documents, but no one can alter them, and they can never be lost.

So what makes cryptocurrency different? Well, the first half of the word, for starters. "Crypto" in this sense comes from the practice known as cryptography, which is a word dating back to the 19th century and a practice used since the time of Julius Caesar.

In general, cryptography is the use of codes, symbols, and algorithms to keep important information safe from unwanted eyes or unintended recipients. It has been used for centuries to pass coded messages between military units, leaders of nations, and leaders of industry. There are tales of famous crypto machines from World War II that saw the Germans encoding their military plans to keep them from being intercepted by the Allies. An entire movie was made about the efforts of British mathematician Alan Turing during World War II to decrypt those messages. Leading actors Benedict Cumberbatch and Keira Knightley received Academy Award nominations for their roles in the film, called "The Imitation Game". In the modern world, cryptography is heavily tied to moving digital information from one person to another. This is often done through the process of encryption to avoid messages being intercepted by a third party. Most emails use a standard form of encryption to give client messages protection. Cryptography relies on a matching set of keys—one that sets the system used and the other unlocks it. Without both, the message is unreadable and usable. In cryptocurrency, the crypto means that cryptography is used to secure online transactions, which makes it nearly impossible for anyone to cheat the system.

What is quite interesting is that the idea of cryptocurrency came to life only after the first cryptocurrency—Bitcoin—was invented in 2008.

In one of the most curious mysteries of the 21st century, Bitcoin was introduced in 2008 by the anonymous inventor known as Satoshi Nakamoto. Why do we call him anonymous if he has a real name? Because it is just a pseudonym, there is no one by that name. Even now, more than a decade after that first revelation, no one has actually admitted to being Nakamoto.

Nakamoto, whether it was a person or a group, registered the website bitcoin.org in August 2008. About two months later, a whitepaper called "Bitcoin: A Peer-to-Peer Electronic Cash System" appeared on a cryptographic mailing list listing Nakamoto as the author. Two months after that, the Bitcoin software was released as open-source code, meaning anyone could view it and expand on the code. The mysterious Nakamoto wrote about the need for a "system for electronic transactions without relying on trust." On January 3, 2009, Nakamoto mined what is called the "genesis block" of Bitcoin which had a value of 50 bitcoins. One of the first supporters of Bitcoin, Hal Finney downloaded the software a week later and received a payment of 10 bitcoins from Nakamoto. This is the first documented transaction of cryptocurrency.

The missing link was removing the central authority by making all the cryptocurrency's users responsible for the system's security. That's where the cryptography comes in. When a cryptocurrency user wants to move funds to another user or to purchase something, they perform a transaction. If Peter wants to give Ellie 2 bitcoin for her birthday, the transaction is made known to the entire network, sent from Peter to every other person using Bitcoin. This is called peer-to-peer (p2p technology). Once the transaction is circulated to all users, it must be verified by all of them before it becomes official. There is no physical exchange of currency, the transaction exists only in the network and the supply is not determined by the central bank because there is not one. Until the transaction is confirmed by all users, it is still pending. Once it has been confirmed, it cannot be altered, which means there is zero risk of anyone ever trying to use the same funds twice for two different transactions.

The most important thing about Nakamoto's invention was that it was the first decentralized digital cash system, which meant that there was no third party dictating rules to the users. Over time, many people have come to distrust the idea of keeping their money in a bank for another financial instrument when they know those institutions are influenced by larger outside sources, namely each country's government. His white paper claims he had tried to build a digital cash system without a central agency for most of the previous decade but failed, thus leading to his decision to invent something different.

Let's take a closer look at Nakamoto's revolutionary white paper:

It was published in 2008 and called "Bitcoin: A Peer-to-Peer Electronic Cash

System." Bitcoin.com offers a simpler explanation of the highlights of the paper, but more in-depth analysis has been done by many experts, students, and other curious parties throughout the last 13 years. In the following breakdowns, the actual text of the whitepaper is italicized and in quotes, with commentary in plain text to follow.

The whitepaper starts off with a simple statement that has been revered and repeated countless times throughout the last decade-plus: *"A purely peer-to-peer version of electronic cash would allow online payment to be sent directly from one party to another without going through a financial institution."*

Pretty simple, yes? Ironically, neither Bitcoin itself nor the blockchain technology is mentioned in this opening statement. Electronic cash is floated as a solution though, which could be interpreted any number of ways, but the centerpiece of the statement is that it does not involve any financial institution.

The second line in the abstract reads: *"We propose a solution to the double-spending problem using a peer-to-peer network. The network timestamps transactions by hashing them into an ongoing chain of hash-based proof-of-work, forming a record that cannot be changed without redoing the proof-of-work."*

Now we're seeing familiar territory, namely the idea behind blockchain technology that, when done right, prevents it from being altered or cheated. It is a simple concept, but not so simple when you consider how Internet-equipped devices work. We can't send money on our desktops, laptops, tablets, or smartphones the way we send a forwarded email, an MP3, or an animated gif file. Why? Because we're not really sending the file, we're sending a copy of it that our computer makes when we attach it to an email or text. That way, we don't lose the original copy; it remains on our system in the exact place we got it from, while the copy gets sent along to its next destination. There's the disparity between real-world transactions and electronic ones. In the real world, if you have a painting I want to buy, I make you an offer and you accept. Then I pay the money and you turn the painting over in exchange for the funds. You don't make a copy of the painting and give me that while keeping the original for yourself. That doesn't make any sense and is not what I paid for. That's the problem with the concept of electronic cash—it's a digital file which means it's easy to copy. So, if I were to send you a digital file worth $100, it would not be that difficult for me to make a copy of that file and send it to you while keeping the original $100 file myself. Then when two of them show up, the typical way it works would see the original take precedence over the copy and my file continue to exist while yours goes away. Clearly that is a huge problem, and the basis of the term "double-spending." When electronic cash exchanges first came into vogue, this was solved by using an intermediary such a PayPal or Visa or something similar to ensure that when Party A sent the $100 to Party B, the money disappeared from Party A's account. Of course, the intermediary made its money by taking a fractional cut of the amount being spent, which meant both parties got a little less in the end.

The anonymity of blockchain and cryptocurrency was something that the eponymous Satoshi appears fanatical about. He wanted to eliminate intermediaries and any personal data that would be collected during a transaction. This notion has, of course, led to some of both blockchain and crypto's problems, notably that criminals have used the technologies for moving funds anonymously. The entire Ransomware trend of the 2010s was based on the fact that hackers could demand ransom in bitcoin that was untraceable to their actual locations or identities.

"What is needed is an electronic payment system based on cryptographic proof instead of trust, allowing any two willing parties to transact directly with each other without the need for a trusted third party. Transactions that are computationally impractical to reverse would protect sellers from fraud, and routine escrow mechanisms could easily be implemented to protect buyers."

It's a little cold-hearted, but undeniably true. Trusting each other with money is simply not a good policy, particularly once you get outside of your own family or circle of friends. So, trust cannot be the end all, and be all of how transitions are made to satisfy both parties. Thus, another system is needed, one that would be safe from fraud and able to lock each transaction as it happened. While the mathematics and ideas behind cryptographic proofs of trust is often where people' eyes glaze over when they are talking about blockchain and cryptocurrency, this is not a new technology. Cryptographic proofs are used to authenticate many forms of digital communications over the Internet, most notably HTTPS—since 1994—and PGP email encryption, which debuted in 1991.

"We define an electronic coin as a chain of digital signatures. Each owner transfers the coin to the next by digitally signing a hash of the previous transaction and the public key of the next owner, and adding these to the end of the coin. A payee can verify the signatures to verify the chain of ownership."

There's a fairly steep uptick here in terms of language and the math required to understand it. There is no actual coin despite what the message says. The coin is a record of ownership, rather like if you were to sign a dollar bill before you gave it to the sales clerk, who then signs it to let the next person know she received it and took ownership of it. Over time you could track the dollar's entire history based on each of the signatures attached to it.

"We need a way for the payee to know that the previous owners did not sign any earlier transactions. For our purposes, the earliest transaction is the one that counts, so we don't care about later attempts to double-spending. The only way to confirm the absence of a transaction is to be aware of all transactions."

Instead of it being $1 that you're giving to a clerk, imagine you're giving them a check for $50. The check has three specific numbers on it: your bank account, your routing number, and a check number. Two of those three things stay the same for every check you write, while the third fluctuates. So if you wrote a check for $50 to pay for your purchases at the grocery store, the bank ledger would show that Check #001 had been spent and could not be duplicated. If three weeks later you forged a second Check #001 for $500 to buy a new television, it would catch in the system that this was an attempt at double-spending and would be rejected.

"The solution we propose begins with a timestamp server. A timestamp

server works by taking the hash of a block of items to be time stamped and widely publishing the hash, such as in a newspaper of Usenet post."

It tells you just how long ago 2008 was when we get a Usenet post reference. But seriously, hashtag data is very useful as a failsafe for data's integrity. The algorithm will have a fixed-length output every time it is run, so there is no massive space being eaten up by bigger files. Even more important is the fact that if anything is changed in the slightest in the original data, it will change the output file, making it instantly obvious that a breach has occurred. Since the original file holds the highest value in blockchain, the second instance of it will not be validated or published and whatever changes were being attempted will not occur.

"To implement a distributed timestamp server on a peer-to-peer basis, we will need to use a proof-of-work system... which involves scanning for a value that when hashed, the hash begins with a number of zero bits. The average work required is exponential to the number of zero bits required and can be verified by executing a single hash."

If that last bit—pardon the pun—flew over your head a little, don't worry, you're not alone. The simplified idea is that each transaction must be confirmed by the network so that everyone concurs it is a valid translation and worthy of joining the blockchain. Transactions are grouped together into blocks. Computers then add junked code to the equation in an effort to find a hash value that begins with the same number of zeroes. This work is done to ensure that no outsiders can influence the block of transactions. Once the hash is found, anyone on the network with input data can verify its accuracy.

"Once the CPU effort has been expended to make it satisfy the proof-of-work, the block cannot be changed without redoing the work. As later blocks are chained after it, the work to change the block would include redoing all the blocks after it."

These two sentences are the landmark principle for blockchain, the technology that many people feel is the real value item in the Bitcoin/cryptocurrency mad rush on the stock market. Part of the input data for each block references the block that came before it. It is impossible to alter the transactions of a past block without recalculating the hash value of every block that comes after it, since altering the data would make progressive changes down the line. The older the block is, the more power it takes to compute the change, meaning the more difficult it becomes to change the record, particularly without someone else noticing it and clamping down on your efforts.

"The steps to run the network are as follows:
1. *New transactions are broadcast to all nodes.*
2. *Each node collects new transactions into a block.*
3. *Each node works on finding a difficulty proof-of-work for its block.*
4. *When a node finds a proof-of-work, it broadcasts the block to all nodes.*
5. *Nodes accept the block only if all transactions in it are valid and not already spent.*
6. *Nodes express their acceptance of the block by working on creating the next block in the chain, using the hash of the computer block as the previous hash."*

Here things can differ, but math still wins out. Nakamoto. Notice that Step #4 says that nodes find "a" proof-of-work, not necessarily "the" proof-of-work. There may be occasions where there is more than one proof that matches the given block, which leads to two different branches being formed on the blockchain. As other nodes join the fray, they will add to one block or the other. Eventually one will become longer than the other, at which point the shorter branch is tossed aside and the longer one joins the block.

"By convention, the first transaction in a block is a special transaction that starts a new coin owned by the creator of the block. The steady addition of a constant of coins is analogous to gold miners expending resources to add gold to circulation. In our case, it is CPU time and electricity that is expended."

Translation? If you don't take part in the process, you don't get the reward of gaining bitcoins. It is the reward for finding the hash value of the transactions. Of course, Nakamoto envisioned lots of dedicated users doing those computations on personal computers. That has evolved into enormous industrial operations to do professional mining that generates more bitcoins thanks to enormous processing power. With bitcoin breaking $50,000 in March 2020, finding those hexes is bigger business than ever.

Now past its 12th birthday, this 12-part white paper has become the gospel for a generation of cryptocurrency buyers, sellers, and entrepreneurs. What has changed in the evolution of Bitcoin from its originator's vision?

Centralization of mining: Decentralization was a key to Nakamoto's vision, in fact there is nothing he wanted more than a decentralized network. But companies and investment blocks with enough resources have built giant mining facilities to put a large power source for the cryptocurrency in the hands of just a few.

Incentives: Individual miners were supposed to be empowered by the ability to gain bitcoin rewards. Mining now takes heavy-duty equipment, copious amounts of electricity, and just as much cooling ability.

Size of the block: Nakamoto wanted relatively small blocks. As of February 21, 2021, the blockchain's size was 321 GB; not exactly something you can store at your retail outlet desktop.

Privacy: What started as an ideal quickly became a liability as anonymous bitcoin transactions led to dark web sites like the Silk Road, the rise of ransomware, and all kinds of heists that left investors ruined when exchanges couldn't say who had walked off with millions of bitcoins. You have to work hard to stay anonymous online these days. Bitcoin is so big that it is traded in centralized exchanges that require IDs. Not exactly an anonymous club anymore.

The real key to the reason that cryptocurrency exists and one of the reasons so many people invest in it is the technology behind it, which is called blockchain.

Chapter 2
Defining Blockchain

Mastering blockchain's ins and outs can be challenging because there is no physical representation of it; it all happens on a network of computers.

Each transaction that occurs is stored as a block. For instance, if Madelyn agrees to rent her garage apartment to Lily for $100/month, when Lily pays the first $100, that transaction is recorded and stored in a block. Every time Lily pays another month's rent, a new block is added and connected to the one before it. All the blocks form an irreversible chain that is transparent to the two parties involved. It would be impossible for Madelyn to say that Lily missed a month's rent or for them to say they accidentally paid twice one month because all transactions are visible for both parties to see and cannot be altered.

If you've ever used Google Docs or Google Sheets, you are a step closer to understanding blockchain. Google Docs allows multiple users access to the same document at the same time. Blockchain allows all members to view any blocks simultaneously.

In the world of cryptocurrency, blockchain is the perfect ledger system because all users are aware of all transactions: nothing is going on 'under the table'.

But blockchain is more than just a storage tool. Its security hinges on the ledger being distributed and encrypted along the network's users and devices. A new device cannot access the network without being authenticated by the whole ledger.

What else can blockchain do? Advocates of the technology would suggest the better question is: What can't blockchain do? The possibilities are nearly unlimited, but for now let's consider a few possibilities.

Blockchain can validate anything. Whether it's sales for your online store or the authentication of votes in a local election, the fears of cloud security are real, just ask any of the giant corporations that have taken massive data hits in the past decade (Target, Yahoo!, Equifax, etc.). Because of the structure it is based upon, blockchain offers a safe environment to store valuable information.

It can manage smart contracts. With a few lines of code, a blockchain-secured smart contract can secure the parameters of any agreement and be the objective executor of that contract once certain requirements are met.

For instance, say you own a beach house that you rent out to tourists each summer. You employ a housekeeping service to clean it and to leave the key in a certain location when a new renter is coming to stay. The smart contract can be written to say that the key will not be placed until the renter has deposited $250 into your PayPal account. When the deposit happens, the smart contract's opening parameter is fulfilled and a message is sent to your contact at the housekeeping service to release the key. The contract can have another agreement in place that requires the housekeeping service to confirm that the key has been returned and there is no damage to the property before the deposit is returned to the renter.

It can be your non-bank. Let's face it, banks have turned a lot of people off in the last decade, between their role in the collapse of the housing bubble and their fee system to make money off services that used to be free. Whether you are using cryptocurrency as your main source of buying things or if you have put your money in another service like Google Wallet, Blockchain can keep track of your funds digitally and incorporate apps on your smartphone when you want to make a payment or add a direct deposit.

It takes out the middleman. You have a great song you wrote on the piano. You play it at coffee houses and get signed to a label. A company wants to use it in a commercial, but first they have to get the label's permission and sign a contract with the label. Your percentage of profit every time the commercial is somewhere between diddly and squat. With Blockchain, you set up a smart contract with the ad agency doing the commercial. It's transparent and neither side can alter the contract without the other's permission.

What Concerns Does Blockchain Have?

For starters, the **blockchain security is not foolproof**. In the summer of 2016, Hong Kong's bitcoin exchange Bitfinex lost about $70 million in customer currency as the result of a hack that still hasn't been fully explained. Even worse the value of those bitcoins had increased to a value around $730 million by November of 2017.

The **sheer number of cryptocurrencies** also raises a red flag for blockchain's success. According to Coin Market Cap, there were 7,800 cryptocurrencies in existence at the end of 2020. Interoperability between that many different currencies, not to mention all the fiat currencies held by countries all over the world, is an enormous task, and not one easily solved.

And regulations might be the issue that really limits blockchain, particularly when it's used to conduct financial transactions. You might not be a bank, but if you are acting as a business and selling wares or services in the US to another individual or company, there are any number of regulations that both you and the system you are using must fall in compliance with to operate legally in the US.

Cryptocurrency is already being given a thorough shakedown by the US Congress and the SEC. Blockchain will surely fall under the same scrutiny as more people use it to move money, services and sales.

Whether you're using blockchain or not, there's no denying its usage is on the rise and is just now scratching the surface of what it can do for individuals, businesses and governments. Its strengths—transparency, security and a reduction of red tape—are essential to the speed of business that the digital age has brought to our world.

Chapter 3
Exposing Cryptocurrency and Blockchain Myths

As with anything new, there is going to be a lot of false information spread about cryptocurrency and blockchain, just as there was for the Internet, social media, and even the year 2,000 (Y2K will cause planes to fall from the sky!). Here are some of the most well-believed myths about the two technologies that need to be put out of their misery.

Myth: The cryptocurrency market is a bubble that is about to burst.

Facts: In the last 10 years, cryptocurrency is the world's top-performing asset class at around $1.3 trillion. It is the world's fifth-most circulated currency in the same time frame, despite only being around since 2010. Many experts are calling it the sequel to gold in the digital age and think it has helped drive the digital economy as well as spur on the fourth Industrial Revolution. Just year over year from 2020 to 2021, there has been a 3,800% increase in value to crypto as an asset class. As a comparison, gold rose 25% in that same period.

Myth: There is only one blockchain.

Facts: There is at least one blockchain per cryptocurrency. Every crypto has its own style and code, but every single one is built on the theory of blockchain technology recording transactions and adding new blocks of information every 10 minutes or so. Blockchains exist based on their purpose and industry. Some are private, others are public. Some are closed-source, others are open-source. One of the biggest struggles for crypto getting universal adoption is that the blockchains have no common denominator. If you have bitcoin and I have ether, we can't trade one for the other and have the transaction show up in both blockchain instances. It would be like going to a restaurant in China and trying to pay with Mexican pesos. We all agree it's a form of currency, but it's not worth squat in the Chinese restaurant.

Myth: Blockchain is only good for digital assets like crypto.

Fact: Absolutely not! In fact many experts and investors will suggest that blockchain is by far the more appealing investment of the two in the long run because it has so many applications in the real world, it's just a matter of getting people to buy into them. Ethereum's smart contracts are the living proof of this, and a big reason why top investors like Mark Cuban are more bullish on the No. 2 cryptocurrency in terms of market value rather than the almighty bitcoin. For organizations and industries where transparency and security surpass profit margins, blockchain is a very viable option. It has been used in counting votes in elections, in maintaining health records for hospitals, in recording donations for nonprofits, and to seal contracts like property acquisitions and deals for recording artists.

Myth: Crypto does not have any intrinsic value.

Fact: Cryptos do not need to be backed by a commodity holding value. This is probably the biggest disconnect that most people have with crypto. They can't see it, so they think it's not real. It is a struggle for many because we place so much importance on the tangibility of something. A US $20 in your wallet has a feel, a smell, and a visual appeal for anyone holding it. You can't hold a bitcoin in your hand. But the $20 bill is only a piece of paper with a picture of a dead president and some fancy anti-tampering ink drawn on it. The US Federal Reserve estimates it costs about 11.2 cents to print a $20 bill, which means that its worth as a physical commodity is thousands of times less than its worth in a department store. Being able to separate the item from its value is the first major step in understanding what crypto is. The second is to envision the relationship between your paycheck and your bank account. A majority of people don't ever see their weekly pay in the form of coins and bills delivered to their hands by their supervisors on payday. Most people get either a paper check or a receipt showing their money has been sent via direct deposit to a bank account of their choice. They check their balance to ensure it's in the account and all they see is a number with a dollar sign in front of it. There's no tangible representation of what just happened other than a figure on a screen. While it would be possible for the person to go to the bank and request the entire check be withdrawn into dollars and cents they could physically hold in their hands, that almost never happens, because digital transactions are so widely accepted and convenient. A tired old argument is that fiat currencies, such as cash, are more valuable than crypto because they are backed by commodities such as gold or silver. But we know that this has not been the case for decades. The only thing fiat currency is backed by is the fact that it was issued by a government and that it's been agreed upon by that government and merchants and customers to be used to buy and sell goods and services of the same value. Break that down even farther and you'll notice that people would be able to work the exchange service out easily without the government's involvement. Does your Congressman have to be standing by when you buy a bucket of popcorn for $6 at the movie theater to make sure everything's on the up and up? Of course not, you and the person at the snack bar are perfectly capable of handling the deal yourself. If people can set the exchange rate by themselves for transactions, what is the government needed for? This simple idea was the genesis of the creation of crypto in the first place. Crypto operates similarly, the agreement is in the place of willing buyers and sellers, the same rules of supply and demand that have been holding economies together for thousands of years. The fact that there is not a tangible asset has lost most of its power in the world. Think about Facebook, which has been valued at more than $750 billion. Can you go on Facebook and buy a product? Can you ask for Facebook to come by your house and cut the grass or clean the gutters? Facebook holds worth in its network, the way it connects people, and how advertisers can harness those connections. It is impossible to hold a Facebook product in your hand or to tell someone "Get your hands off my Facebook!" Crypto also holds value because of the concept of scarcity, that is, it is limited in nature. At some point Bitcoin will reach its maximum number of coins, at which point the only way to acquire more is to buy it from someone. There will only be 21 million bitcoins ever produced.

Myth: Crypto is only used for illicit activities.

Fact: Far more illegal transactions are paid for in fiat currency than cryptocurrencies. It takes a lot of work to put dangerous transactions on the blockchain, as technology in the present has greatly improved when it comes to security. Only 0.5% of bitcoin transactions in 2019 were done on the dark web according to a Bitcoin Laundering report put out by the US government. This number has come down dramatically since the early days of crypto trading. As bigger and bigger organizations get involved in crypto, cybersecurity increases. Global policies like Know Your Customer (KYC) and Know Your Transactions (KYT) make transactions under false names and false pretenses a thing of the past in most countries. There are still some cryptocurrencies designed strictly for anonymous transactions, but they total just 0.01% of the overall market value of crypto.

Myth: Crypto is unregulated.

Fact: Crypto regulation is on the rise in every corner of the world, including major players like the EU, UK, US, and China. The US has been back and forth on how to classify and tax crypto for years (see more information on this later in this text) with 2021 starting to give a little clarity as Washington DC is finally seeing an influx of politicians and officials with actual interest and experience in crypto. The biggest fear in the early days of crypto was that governments would out and out ban the entire industry, but today there are 13 countries where crypto is considered a legal tender, including Japan, Australia, and several EU nations. Australia is also transitioning to a blockchain system by April 2022 for its Securities Exchange. In the private sector, Amazon has been the first major player to start accepting crypto for payment, with Microsoft, Dell, Expedia, Twitch, and Fiverr joining the fray a bit later.

Myth: Elon Musk invented Bitcoin.

Fact: Even he says he didn't. We'll get to Musk quite a bit more later in this book, but the billionaire leader of Tesla and SpaceX is certainly a good candidate to link to Bitcoin, given his status as a computer whiz kid and his habit for ground-breaking technology. Bitcoin was invented by someone using the alias Satoshi Nakamoto, with the real architect never actually coming forth despite many theories over the years of who it was. The fact that a real person has never come forward has been one of the hangups that a lot of people have when it comes to investing in cryptocurrency in general.

How can you trust something when you don't really know where it came from?

Myth: Bitcoin is not taxed.

Fact: That might have been true early on, but most countries' tax authorities have wised up in the last 5-7 years and started taxing it just like any other asset, meaning you get taxed for possessing it, and taxed when you sell it. The US in particular has had a supreme identity crisis on how exactly to classify and tax crypto holdings, with its Internal Revenue Service and Securities Exchange Commission muddying the waters further by coming up with contradictory definitions. The US is among a number of countries trying to get citizens to pay back taxes on gains made in crypto before it was being regulated. You can guess how that process is currently going. However, countries are starting to crack down more and more on those who try to avoid paying taxes on crypto, putting pressure on exchanges to regulate the process and performing audits more and more often.

Myth: There is an unlimited amount of bitcoin.

Fact: Not so fast! based on the way the system is made, there can be no more than 21 million bitcoin mined. As of May 2021, that number was at 18.6 million (about 88.5% of capacity), but don't worry about missing out if you haven't gotten any. Because of the high price of bitcoin, mining new ones takes an immense amount of time. Experts don't expect the maximum number to be reached until at least 2100.

Myth: There are fewer than 100 cryptocurrencies.

Fact: Not even close. As of May 2021 there were more than 4,000 currencies in circulation, although even the most astute of crypto experts is unlikely to be able to name more than about 20 at any time. Why are there so many? Well, because like any other industry where it looks like you can make money with a little bit of an investment, people have flocked to crypto over the years. To create a coin, you don't need an office, a financial backer, or even business cards; just a programmer or two who knows how to write code and get you a website like GoFundMe or in front of an angel investor or two. Most are destined to fail, much like most startups won't make it past the five-year mark. Some cryptos are smart enough to allow others to be built on their networks, which makes the newer models seem like they are backed by the originals, such as Ethereum. Others are based in apps that are churned out and dropped unceremoniously into the Apple or Google Play stores to collect dust until something goes viral or a true worth for it is found.

Myth: You can't buy anything with bitcoin

Fact: Even though Musk has made headlines for disallowing bitcoin as a payment for Tesla products, otherwise it's quite untrue. You can even receive your salary in bitcoin in parts of the world, and PayPal and Amazon are both accepting more than a few cryptocurrencies as payments on their websites. What other major players are on the list? How about Microsoft, Overstock, Dish Network, Subway, every site on Shopify, Expedia, Pizzaforcoins, Reeds Jewelers, Intuit Services, and eGifter?

Myth: Cryptocurrencies will take the place of the dollar.

Fact: Bitcoin has been around for 11 years and has dropped as much as 50% in a single day because of one person's tweet. The dollar has been around since the US began and has survived two world wars, a presidential impeachment, a civil war, corruption at the highest levels, and Donald Trump as president. Investors continue to believe in the dollar even in tough times like during the Great Recession of 2008-2010 and the recent COVID-19 pandemic. Domestic and foreign investors are routinely purchasing trillions of dollars in US Treasury securities even with fairly low interest rates. While crypto is unlikely to make even a sizable dent in the dollar's prowess during any of our lifetimes, it is an exciting, viable alternative option, which is what most people who invest in it really want—a way to put their money somewhere else that isn't so directly tied to the whims and wagers of governments around the world. It doesn't have to take over the world, but giving people a choice is a very democratic system of finance.

Myth: Cryptocurrencies are a fad that will vanish over time.

Fact: Warren Buffet, the billionaire American investment adviser, once compared crypto to the 17th century tulip craze. Tulips were first sent to Europe from the Ottoman Empire in the 16th century and became a huge hit in Belgium and The Netherlands, having never been seen before Europeans had the same reaction to their first experiences with peppers, potatoes, tomatoes, and other vegetables. Tulips were very different from other flowers native to Europe due to their intense colors. They became a huge status symbol as Amsterdam and other cities began churning out ships headed to the East Indies to acquire more. These ships could sometimes make up to 400% profit on the loads they returned. Growers of tulips specialized in specific colors and started giving them extravagant names like "Admiral of Admirals" and "General of Generals". By 1636, the flower had become so popular in France that tulip bulbs were the Netherlands' fourth most popular export product, trailing only gin, fish, and cheese. Tulip futures became a commodity to be traded in, even by people who had never actually seen a tulip. During 1636 and 1637, tulip bulb contracts were changing hands as many as 10 times a day, but the whole thing came lurching to a halt when an outbreak of the bubonic plague occurred in the city of Haarlem and buyers refused to show up to bid on bulbs at auction. The plague burst the bubble as people suddenly clung to their money like it was the only piece of wood in the middle of the ocean following a shipwreck. At its peak, a single bulb could be traded for a silver drinking cup, twelve fat sheep, four fat oxen, eight fat pigs, two tons of butter, four tons of beer, or 1,000 pounds of cheese.

Andrew Bailey, Bank of England Governor, echoed Buffett's opinion by saying that British citizens should invest in crypto only if they were "prepared to lose all your money" and economist Noruiel Roubini once called Bitcoin either the "mother or father of all scams". Of course, two of those people oversee massive amounts of money and have responsibilities to keep people investing in the funds that they have created. If Buffett, who spent decades building up trust for his investors in oil and gas stocks, technology, and staple goods, suddenly told them all to buy crypto because it was the best thing ever, there'd be a kind of panic that would make the Stock Market Crash of 1929 seem like mild indigestion after a big lunch. Fear of the unknown is a detriment to any new technology. Record executives bashed the CD like it was made of poison and did likewise when digital downloads started popping up online. The Internet itself was seen as a passing fad, most famously (and hilariously) by author Clifford Stoll, who in 1995 said the Internet would be dead by the end of 1996. Stoll's piece, which included memorable gaffes like "the truth is no online database will replace your daily newspaper" and "You can't tote a laptop to the beach." have made the rounds for years as an example of how no technology should be doubted before it has a chance to breathe. If anything, crypto should be taken seriously because of the caliber of minds who are invested in it, both financially and mentally. Would the likes of Musk, Zuckerberg, and Cuban be blindly throwing their money away on an industry that is destined to fail? You don't get to be a billionaire by repeatedly swinging and missing.

Buffett continues to be the outlier, telling CNBC in 2020 that he doesn't own crypto, and he never will. His reason is three-fold. First, he thinks it is an unproductive asset. "They can't reproduce, they can't mail you a check, they can't do anything, and what you hope is that somebody else comes along and pays more money for them later on, but then that person's got the problem." His second problem is that he doesn't think it counts as real money, calling it a "mirage", and thirdly, he doesn't understand it. That's the real linchpin here. No investor in the world is going to endorse something he doesn't understand, at least not any self-respecting one. "I get in enough trouble with things I think I know something about," Buffett quips. "Why in the world should I take a long or short position in something I don't know anything about?" Fortunately, there are other top investors that are a little more pliable with their ability to see crypto's potential, who are all in on the investment.

Myth: Every blockchain is public

Facts: Big factors in the success of blockchain technology is that they are transparent, but that doesn't mean they need to have public access. Private and hybrid blockchains are just as popular and useful depending on what your need is. For instance, a hospital might put patient healthcare files in a blockchain format to protect them and ensure they are not altered, but the files in the blockchain must be kept secure for privacy's sake. Putting such information on a blockchain would violate a ton of privacy laws, so a private blockchain makes perfect sense.

Myth: Blockchains cannot be hacked.

Facts: Unfortunately, that's not true. If it were, we'd probably be a whole lot closer to universal acceptance and embracing of blockchain and crypto right now. Blockchain tech is based on encryption of information between two parties. That encryption is known as the SHA-256 cryptographic hash algorithm, which can really scramble up files to the point where it's next to impossible to unscramble them without the encryption key. The only way to truly break it would be via brute force, which means have a computer run through every possible combination. Unless you get lucky, that might take a few decades or a century or two, though. However, some hackers and cybercriminals are able to figure out what the original algorithm was that is the progenitor for the encryption. If that is pulled, it becomes possible to make the blockchain vulnerable and it can be compromised at a much faster rate. In essence, what cyberthieves are looking for when they go after a blockchain is human error. That is what gives them the possibility of cracking the encryption. In 2019 alone, there were 12 cryptocurrency hacks that resulted in 500,000 pieces of customer data and $292 million being stolen. The number actually dropped in 2020 to 12 hacks for $5.91 million total, the first time the number has fallen in the past five years.

Myth: Blockchain exists on the cloud

Fact: It does exist there, but you should not rely on cloud-based databases to manage something as important as your crypto. Download the crypto app of your choice and run it on your Internet-enabled computer to become a node for the blockchain being run by whatever currency you happen to own. The stronger your connection is and the more CPU power you have available to do computations, the stronger the network is.

Myth: All blockchain transactions are anonymous.

Facts: Not anymore, they aren't. The anonymity of the early incarnations of blockchain was too good to be true, particularly for drug dealers, terrorists, and other black-market personnel. Why do you think so many ransomware scams were successful a few years ago? Now the blockchain only records the public addresses of wallets avoiding disclosure on the name of the wallet owner. The technology was limited in the earlier years because people weren't expecting criminals to fly in a frenzy to crypto as a way to circumvent the law and move goods, services, laundered money, drugs, and everything else under the sun. Law enforcement was ill equipped to prevent or investigate this sort of behavior in the early days of crypto; its technology was light years behind the time.

Myth: Blockchain is free

Facts: No, it is not, although the primary cost is in the use of the computers that power the mathematical equations to prove transactions are valid. This has become increasingly a point of contention over time as the number of transactions has skyrocketed, and with it the amount of electricity being used in cryptocurrency. In an era when mechanical, industrial, and other industries are all under strict guidelines around the world to reduce their carbon footprints to preserve the environment, keep average temperatures down, and make a better tomorrow for our children, cryptocurrency mining is in need of serious reform to lower costs and the pollution associated with mining. With the enemies crypto and blockchain have already made from governments surrounding the world that are distrustful of its intent and its value, the last thing that fans of the industry want is to add to the negative opinion by letting the electrical consumption go unchecked. In some countries, including Iran, there is so much unchecked electrical crypto mining that the power grids are experiencing blackouts. Even now, Ethereum and other major players in the crypto/blockchain market are seeking ways to cut down on their power drain to cut costs and avoid costly penalties from various environmental protection agencies. The yet-to-be released Ethereum 2.0 is supposed to be the first look at this model.

Chapter 4
The Economic Theory of Cryptocurrency and the Cashless Society

The average American has been sluggish to embrace cryptocurrency as a valid form of payment. The reasons behind that are many, some psychological, some academic, some downright superstitious. What is at the root of this mistrust? The most fundamental reason is that the economics of cryptocurrency are misunderstood by an overwhelming number of average people, but then again, the theory of currency itself is not either.

Let's start with the basics, which is that for just about every person alive in the United States today, currency has two physical forms: metal coins and paper dollars.

Except that we don't use physical currency nearly as much as we used to, do we? If you take a trip to the grocery store and watch the head of household rack up $278 worth of kids' lunches, deli meat, soda, dog food, and ice cream, they don't often get out their wallet or purse and start counting out $20 bills, quarters, and nickels, do they?

It's a sign of the times. In 2019, the Diary of Consumer Payment Choice, a product of the Federal Reserve, found that for the first time in US history, cash was no longer responsible for the largest percentage of monetary transactions in the US.

Debit cards rose to 28% of payments in the study, with cash falling to second at 26%. In the next few years, cash stands likely to drop to third in that chase, as already 23% of all transactions were made on credit cards. So there's already an interesting contradiction of terms. People claim not to trust cryptocurrency because they cannot see or hold it. Yet 51% of transactions for the entire country were made using credit and debit cards, which have no more value in their physical form than a straw or a roll of toilet paper. People are paying fewer transactions per month in cash—about 11 at the time of this survey—and it is only responsible for 10% of transactions of $25 or more. So, the paper currency that we all grew up craving in a birthday card from our grandmother or thrilled to find at the bottom of the swimming pool is a very small percentage of the actual supply of money in the world. Most of the money supply currently resides in the form of credit or simply as electronic figures inside banking systems.

Paper currency got its start in the US in 1690, issued by the Massachusetts Bay Colony for the purpose of paying soldiers of fortune to take on military expeditions to scout the surrounding area or fend off hostile Native Americans. The first official currency in US history were paper notes issued by the Continental Congress to fund the American army. Of course, the money only went as far as the backing behind it, and the fact that the backing was a bunch of traitors funding an army that went through years of stalemates and setbacks, and it's not hard to see why people started using the phrase that something wasn't "worth a Continental."

Over the next 50 years, the US experimented with all sorts of notes for different purposes, such as paying taxes or buying specific goods.

In 1791, Alexander Hamilton established the Bank of the United States, primarily to give the US government a line of credit. A year later, the Mint Act was passed to establish a coinage system. It took almost another century for US currency to start looking the way it does now—with a central printing and engraving department, George Washington on the $1 bill, and all paper currency backed by the silver standard. In 1879, the US switched from the silver standard to the gold standard.

In 1913, President Woodrow Wilson enacted the Federal Reserve Act that created the nation's central bank that could more easily manipulate the needs of the country. When the US was on the gold standard, the price of gold determined how much a dollar was worth. So if the price of gold was $100 for an ounce, the value of a dollar would be 1/100th of an ounce of gold.

That policy didn't last too long thanks in large part to the Great Depression, which led to people hoarding gold. The British came off their gold standard in 1931, and the US followed suit in 1933. The new style of US currency backing was fiat money—the currency used by the order of the government. The term "fiat" derives for the Latin *fieri*, which means an arbitrary act or decree. So, for a full 88 years there has been no backing for the US currency other than good faith in its government. If every single person decided they all wanted to withdraw their money in cash tomorrow morning, it could not happen, there is simply not enough of the green stuff to go around. Although it has not happened yet, there will soon be Americans who are born and reach adulthood without ever seeing real hard currency like dollar bills, quarters, dimes, and nickels. Outside of the occasional vending machine, there is increasingly less use for it. These are interesting points to make because what is universally accepted for the dollar is seen as a down note for the existence of cryptocurrency.

The US kept a touchstone with gold through 1971 when President Richard Nixon took that offline, fearful of how many foreign countries had large amounts of dollars in their own treasuries that they might have cashed in and sent the US economy headed to the poor house. With no hard commodity as the backing, the currency of the US for the past 50 years has been based on nothing more than faith in the government to honor its debts.

A currency backed by faith sounds an awful lot like what cryptocurrency embodies for its users. Unlike the US dollar of course, cryptocurrency is decentralized, meaning there is no government or central bank behind it, instead it is predicated by what its users believe it to be worth. One of the drawbacks that keeps cryptocurrency from achieving true independence is that it is most well-known for how many dollars it is worth, notably the price of Bitcoin, the original cryptocurrency, and by far the most valuable one.

Cryptocurrency began for most people as the dream of a cashless society. The idea is to stop tying the worth of a currency to one country or one banking system. No middleman in the process means no government telling people how much their money is worth or how, when, and why they can spend it. Consumers are mostly happy with this situation, but those who struggle to keep up with technological developments continue to rely on cash.

Is a Cashless Society Possible?

The potential for a cashless society has been bandied about for as long as the Internet has been around and the digital transformation of so many functions of our society has taken place. Government and many large financial services are already leaning towards a cashless society, which would actually make it seem like something cryptocurrency would not want to be part of given the counterculture movement it seems to represent. There are both benefits and disadvantages to a cashless society using cryptocurrency that must be expounded upon before a real stance can be taken one way or the other.

Advantages include:

1. **Less financial crime.** It's just a basic fact that if there is no cash being carried around in wallets and purses, there's going to be a whole lot less of it stolen. When thieves rob someone in today's society, once they've run off and your cash is now in their possession, it's basically impossible to get it back or even prove how much was taken unless they are caught in the next 10 minutes or so. Debit and credit cards numbers are still stolen all the time using sophisticated algorithms to identify odd transactions really cuts down on that. Plus, users are so aware of their minute-by-minute transactions thanks to banking apps that they can pounce on fraudulent transactions in near to real-time and shut down their cards far more quickly than even 10-20 years ago. The State of Missouri offered a good case in point when it replaced all cash welfare benefits with Electronic Benefit Transfer (EBT) cards. Since a lot of crime happens in neighborhoods where many people are on welfare, a study showed that crime dropped 9.8% statewide after the transition to cashless benefits.

2. **Automatic Paper Trails.** This is a positive that cryptocurrency has been lauding since the beginning thanks to its revolutionary blockchain technology. If you ever watched an episode of The Sopranos, you know that Tony and company successfully laundered millions of dollars by running the cash through a dry-cleaning business. Illegal businesses that operate strictly in cash such as gambling rings and drug cartels will have a much more complicated time doing business when cash is no longer an option, and every transaction has a record behind it. No one is naive enough to believe that would completely stop these types of crime, but it would, at the very least, wipe out a lot of low-level operators

who don't have the funds or the resources to set up some sort of dummy account or false front of a company to move money for illegal activities.

3. **Saving money by not having money:** Yes, that was a confusing headline. But the fact of the matter is that it costs a lot of money to keep printing bills and coins. It costs money for businesses to protect their bills and coins as well as making change and having enough cash on hand. If you've ever owned or worked for a small business, you know the hassle of having to hustle to the local bank before it closes to ensure you have enough cash on hand for the weekend crows.

4. **Seamless world economy.** When you travel to a foreign country, one of the first things you do is head for the currency exchange counter at the airport to figure out how much of your money becomes how much of their money. Without physical currency, those exchange rates are known intuitively through your banking app on your phone or tablet and no more confusion is necessary.

Disadvantages include:

1. **No more privacy.** The big one. Electronic payments are not private. Anything and everything you do online is recorded somewhere. You might trust your payment systems and you might feel you have nothing to hide, but lots of people do not want to have all their transactions "on the grid" where anyone can see them. It means if you stop by Starbucks after leaving the house when you promised your wife you would quit, it's going to be recorded. If you want to tip your yard guy, your cleaning lady, or anyone else, they'll have to get on the system as well. Anyone with a side business that deals in cash will suddenly be accountable for that extra income and taxed for it as well. And all your information will be available online, which heightens the chance of someone getting ahold of it and doing something nefarious. The reality is that thousands if not millions of people in this country exist in a world without a bank account at all, much

less checking and savings accounts, debit cards, and credit cards. Is it right to take away the way they like to live for the efficiency of the rest of us? If people want to live "off the grid", is that not their given right by the Constitution, as long as they are obeying the laws and paying taxes? It is a very debatable conundrum that has had fierce arguments for years.

2. **The risk of hacking.** If you wake up one morning and find your account has been drained of all your funds, what do you do to get it back? How do you know exactly how much was in your account? Who do you call? How do you prove it? Once all money is only available electronically, the number of cybercriminals/hackers will skyrocket and that can be a very dangerous thought. So many people do not know how to effectively use online security that a switch to a cashless society would see online theft explode, at least for a time.

3. **Online banking systems are not perfect.** There are glitches, malfunctions, and mistakes every single day. Those could swing in your favor or leave you without funds at the worst possible time. They also make every single person at the mercy of Internet connectivity and electricity. If one of those two things is out, merchants cannot accept your payment and you cannot check your balance or make or receive any payments. That gets us back to the Stone Age really quickly and is a frightening prospect. Cash carries an inherent power with it that lets people know you can pay for something whether the lights are on or off.

4. **More disparity between social classes.** It's already ugly and it could be a lot worse. For every person who taps their cell phone to pay for something they want to buy online, there's someone who has never owned a smartphone a day in their life and has no intention of doing so any time in the future. Going to a society where everything is done by an Internet-capable device puts an economic floor in place that millions of Americans cannot or will not be able to afford. It's just that simple. An overwhelming

majority of the country has access to a device, but even then, you're putting the burden on everyone to do the same thing the same way or they'll be left out entirely with no way to access their funds, make purchases, or release payments to others.

5. **Payment companies charge fees for every transaction.** Banks might charge you when your account is overdrawn, but they're not tacking on a $1 fee every time you buy a hamburger or a slice of pizza. All payment vendors currently in operation in the US take a slice of the pie every time a transaction happens, and even if it's 5 cents per $100, people are still not going to like giving away their money to a company for a process that has previously been free all their lives. Theoretically, the payment companies would be handling such massive volumes of payments that they could reduce the fee to a fraction of a penny for each transaction, but people will still have a hard time giving away what they believe to be rightfully theirs.

6. **Overspending could get dangerously out of control:** Having access to money you cannot see can result in really bad habits forming and overspending at an epic rate. As a whole, Americans had more than $1 trillion in credit card debt in 2020. That's a result of people spending money they don't have and worrying about it later. A well-known tactic for not overspending is to get cash out from the bank, put it in envelopes for your needs over a week or a month, and then only use the cash for purchases. When you run out of cash, you are done making purchases for that time frame! It's not unlike when casinos went from chips to being able to use a credit or debit card at machines. People quickly lost track of how many swipes they were doing because it was so much easier than having to physically go to the window and request a certain number of chips for an equivalent amount of money.

7. **The danger of negative interest rates.** Sometimes countries will drop interest rates in a move to stimulate an economy, but money losing its purchasing power can be a side effect. If banks aren't

making money from interest, they will seek to remain profitable in other ways, such as increasing or inventing fees to take more money from their customers. In the past, customers could pull money out into cash to avoid these fees. In a cashless society, they would not be able to do the same thing.

A cashless society would change huge swathes of how our world works. Credit cards and debit cards are already a normal part of society, as are person-to-person transfers such as Venmo and PayPal. Those do charge fees, and those fees get steep when you are moving money from one country to another. Mobile apps like Apple Pay are secure and cash-free options, but again it's entering all your personal and financial information into the mouth of a mega-beast, just like Google or Amazon, and then crossing your fingers that they actually respect your privacy like they are supposed to. History has shown that is not always what happens.

Cryptocurrencies and blockchain can be a huge part of a cashless economy because they are already introducing new technology to make the process safe. The large number of cryptocurrencies is good for competition because it keeps firms innovating, which in turn keeps costs low for end-users. To become part of the cashless society, cryptocurrencies must find a way to be stable and safe for users to put their money into them long term as a financial institution. While it is thrilling to watch the price of Bitcoin continue to shatter records, nobody wants to put their money into a form of currency where it can be worth $40,000 per coin one day and $18,000 per coin a week later.

Modern Cashless Societies

Two prominent world powers, Sweden and India, have tried to move towards cashless societies in recent years. The results have been a mixed bag.

In late 2016, India's government banned the 500 and 1,000 rupee cash notes in an attempt to penalize criminals and people who skip paying taxes by handling all their transactions in cash. Thinking it would weed out criminals, in India it did not work, as eventually 99% of these notes were deposited into banks, but they were not traceable, and none were deposited in any sort of massive collection that would have suggested ties to organized crime. There was a brief spike in electronic financial transactions following this activity, but people were back to using cash—albeit in smaller denominations—by the end of 2017.

Sweden is a lot closer to achieving the world's first cashless society. There are shops all over the country that have signs up reading "No Cash Accepted" and in 2019, cash transactions were just 1% of the country's GDP. The last few years have seen cash withdrawals from banks and ATM machines fall by about 10% per year. In the country, cafes, shops and supermarkets are displaying QR codes so customers can simply scan and then pay directly with their smartphones. Sweden has quite the history of financial front-running. The country's first ATM machine debuted in July 1967. The country has jumped ahead of almost every other nation on the globe with its BankID technology. This is a mobile app that lets anyone with a Swedish personal identification number and a bank account to gain access to all existing digital public services, as well as perform online banking and sign contracts.

Given Sweden's relatively small population—10.2 million, about the same as North Carolina—it can assign each person a six-digit code for this task or use their fingerprint on a smartphone. This keeps Swedes from having to remember 50 different passwords for all the services online.

The Swedish lifestyle also has played a large role in the move towards a cashless society. Splitting the bill at dinner is a big social trend, and apps that let people quickly move funds from themselves to another person are all the vogue. Swedes see debt as a threat to friendship and always want to make sure they are squared away before the evening ends. As a hub for financial technology (fintech), Sweden also has seen a lot of innovation and been at the forefront. More than 1,000 Swedes have already taken the next step to willingly having a microchip implanted in their hands that store data including their bank cards, tickets for the morning train commute, or an ID to open the door at their job or residence. These people are not just going cashless, they don't even need a card or a set of keys.

According to Sweden's central bank, the Riksbank, the percentage of Swedes using cash has fallen from 40% a decade ago down to just 9% in 2021. The majority of that 9% is for very small purchases and things bought by senior citizens.

In the United States, the COVID-19 pandemic that began in March 2020 has pushed this country towards a cashless society at a much faster rate than anyone would have predicted before the spread of the coronavirus. Although as of June 2020, 82% of small businesses were still accepting cash, most likely because with the economic downturn they will take any form of payment they can get. But the trends of social distancing and fear of interpersonal engagement has more and more people exploring options that don't involve any sort of touch, particularly with the idea that most cash and coins are already pretty filthy. Paper money is known to be potentially dirtier than a toilet. While bacteria and viruses can live on the average surface for 48 hours, paper can carry the flu virus for a staggering 17 days. The bigger problem in the US is that about 7.1 million American households remain unbanked—meaning they have neither a bank nor a credit union account. While that number is down from 8.4 million in 2017, it still represents more than 2% of the population. Low-income families avoid banks because they struggle to keep a minimum balance and can't keep all the fees that revolve around them. Others distrust banks inherently, have had bad experiences, or simply believe their money should stay with them at all times. Until there is an option that makes the unbanked feel comfortable and secure in having a bank account and no longer needing to physically hold their currency, it is tough to imagine how America will get to a point of being cashless.

To broaden its own appeal and insert itself more into American day-to-day financial society, cryptocurrency might consider being the technology that makes a cashless economy rather than the currency itself. Certainly blockchain could be used to solidify security and record-keeping in a cashless society.

Chapter 5
The Cryptocurrency Revolution

Few American innovators can match the success of Henry Ford, who when asked about how public demand factored into his automotive success, quipped, "If I had asked people what they wanted, they would have said faster horses."

There's no denying the power of understanding what a customer base needs and delivering it to them, but Ford's genius was seeing beyond the restrictions of what was and creating something completely different that not only inspired the marketplace, but fundamentally changed the way in which society was composed.

Ford's famous quote resonates well with the current state of the cryptocurrency industry. Crypto has risen in an era where people were looking for something new without really knowing what it was. Crypto combines elements of a currency that frees users from the big banks, a payment system without fees, and an investment vehicle that fits perfectly into the ever-evolving scope of the digital age.

Ford didn't build the Model T in a day and start mass producing it the following week, with one in every driveway the next month. It took a revolution from the inside out to convince the masses to put their horses back in the pasture and turn to the wonders of the automobile.

That progression is a powerful metaphor for the current cryptocurrency environment. Cryptocurrency and the blockchain technology that powers it are every bit as revolutionary, but at the same time foreign, as the Model T and mass production lines for cars were 110 years ago. By learning from previous world-altering innovations, we can better position ourselves to capitalize on the ones of today.

The Trouble with Transitions

Although it's glazed over in most textbooks, the move from the horse to the automobile was a long and difficult one. It took nearly 50 years for the latter to completely replace the former, and forced change in multiple industries and environments, from the condition of roads to the advancements of maps to an entire new section of laws, including local, state, and federal. If that sounds familiar to cryptocurrency users, it comes as no surprise. Entirely new laws are slowly but surely being put in place to mandate every facet of cryptocurrency. It's a time-consuming process that requires research and bureaucratic red tape at every step. The transportation system of getting funds to and from users to platforms and back is completely new and is constantly being upgraded and refined. And the gradual transition for many from relying on fiat currency and traditional investments to digital currency and investments that can change by the second is going to take some getting used to, just as many Americans struggled to get into the car rather than onto the horse.

New Industries Born

The number of new industries born because of the automobile's advancement is almost too many to comprehend. Consider before the dawn of the automobile, no one had ever considered a car stereo, a body shop, tires, a car wash, or even a gas station. Mr. Ford's genius idea that came rolling faithfully off that assembly line has created billions upon billions of jobs and produced a global industry. Cryptocurrency and blockchain are providing the same opportunities as the industry begins to expand and take shape. From websites to platforms to digital IRAs, and that's just the tip of the iceberg. As more and more enterprises become comfortable with the security and effectiveness of blockchain, it will be one of the more sought-after technologies.

While the average person might believe Henry Ford invented the car (he didn't) and the mass production assembly line for cars (he didn't do that either). Instead he was taking what had been done before, seeing where it had failed, and producing a new version that was not only less expensive, but also faster and better. Ford's product might have angered his competition at first, but it was the best kind of angry; the kind that makes you push yourself to be even better—the kind that drives innovation and competition. More than a century later, the same will hold true and has already begun to happen digitally. While Bitcoin is the most recognizable name in cryptocurrency, this book and the market in general will help you realize that it is far from the case. Other companies have stood on Bitcoin's shoulders to innovate and make remarkable strides in many industries. Think about the modern Tesla compared to the Model-T. Both can get you from Point A to Point B on four tires, but most of the similarities end there. One was meant for short drives with the top down, the other ignores the laws of gasoline and cruises long distances quietly.

Every person who got into a Model T those first few years was guaranteed of one thing: an exhilarating ride on a bumpy road. The comparison is a striking one to the early days of cryptocurrency, where most companies and investors were fumbling around in the dark trying to find the light. There are highs and lows associated with the industry, but incredible opportunities are not only here now, but also visible just over the horizon.

What's Behind Bitcoin's Big Bounce?

We'll go through Bitcoin's extensive history in Chapter 5, but if you're paying attention even a little bit to recent world events, you know that Bitcoin has exploded in price in the first part of the 2020s, defeating all expectations again and again.

The original cryptocurrency first broke the elusive $1,000 price in February 2017. By the end of that year it had risen to $14,000, before tumbling back down to about $3,200 around a year later. Since then it has started to climb relentlessly, with even the catastrophic news of the coronavirus unable to staunch its flow. It was nearly up to $10,000 in February 2020, then tumbled to less than $5,000 in the early confusion of the COVID-19 pandemic. It regained the $10,000 platform in the summer of 2020 and has since been shattering records day after day. It jumped $2,000 to breach $20,000 in December 2020, but that was quickly old news. $30,000 was surpassed on the second day of 2021, five weeks later it fell to $40,000. A remarkable $7,000 was gained over two days later that month and the price has been as high as $54,000 into March 2021. So what in the world is causing such a massive explosion in price? If you put $5,000 into bitcoin in February 2017, you could sell those 5 coins today for $270,000. That's a return on investment of

53,000%.

So what's the mystery formula behind this historic rise? Here are a few of the leading theories.

Institutional buyers hedging versus inflation: Institutional buyers are often companies or organizations committed to invest money for others. They typically take the form of pensions, insurance companies, or mutual funds. In this, they are typically looking for investments that have long-term stability and can weather the storm of the up-and-down trends of the current volatile market. These buyers are often thought of as the whales of Wall Street, meaning they buy massive quantities of stocks, bonds, and other securities they believe will last a long time at a premium value. What drags them down is inflation, such as when the Federal Reserve tries to stimulate the economy by printing more money, when all that actually does is weaken the dollar. The Fed can print more money, but by the original network programming of bitcoin, there can never be more than 21 million coins produced. A limited capacity of a highly sought-after commodity will cause its price to go up and stay up. In January 2021, Investment banking firm JPMorgan put a long-term target price for bitcoin at a staggering $146,000 and called it an alternative currency to gold. This is the same JPMorgan, mind you, whose CEO Jamie Dimon labeled bitcoin a fraud back in 2017.

The dollar's downturn internationally: The US Dollar is the most important currency in the world, and its index gauges its value against other big currencies, such as the Japanese yen or the EU's euro. A lot of that has to do with a reason stated above, the US Federal Reserve has printed more than $3 trillion over the past year, in an era where people are using cash less in an attempt to kickstart an economy that went on lockdown with the rest of the world for much of 2020 due to the coronavirus global pandemic. Even without the presence of COVID-19, it's been a rocky time in the US from the outside looking in. The 2020 Presidential election was a bitter feud that included incumbent Donald Trump insisting the election was rigged and that he was the victim, culminating with thousands of his supporters illegally entering the US Capitol in January on the day that the Congress was due to certify the election results and officially declare Joe Biden the winner. Trump going out and Biden coming in doesn't guarantee any sudden stability either. The Democratic leader has promised new stimulus packages for COVID relief as well as other large spending plans that have good chances of passing since the Democrats also have the majority control of Congress. So much spending might be great for the people directly affected by it, but when those US dollars are put to work without any sort of fiduciary return, the dollar becomes weaker. If your traditional currency isn't looking appealing its alternatives become more appealing.

Retail Purchases: It's becoming easier and easier to use bitcoin to buy everyday items, particularly once PayPal got on-board with the cryptocurrency in 2020. Of course, buying with bitcoin at the present date feels a little like selling your gold bars to buy stuff —sure it's effective as money, but why in the world would you? When it was hovering below $1,000/coin for years, the novelty was certainly there to purchase from local merchants who were trying to expand into cryptocurrencies by accepting them as payment. But if you made a $100 purchase in 2017 with bitcoin — about 1/10th of a coin back then, you're now living with the grief that the $100 you spent has now grown into $5,000 of value. We're guessing the item you bought has not likewise appreciated in the past three years.

Halving: Halving is a process coded into Bitcoin since the beginning that functions as its own escrow mechanism. We have spoken at length about how miners get a reward for their work processing transactions. The reward is cut in half every four years, meaning it is a law of diminishing returns for the miners. That means the rate of inflation is reduced by half every four years and will continue to do so until all bitcoin in the escrow is released. That will happen when Bitcoin caps at 21 million coins. There are currently about 18.5 million in circulation. Despite appearing near capacity, the timeline is a good deal more complicated. Since the halving keeps taking place, the rewards for mining a new block will continue to go down significantly. When Bitcoin was first launched, the reward was 50 bitcoins. In February 2021, it was down to 6.25 bitcoins. Most estimates say the last bitcoin won't be mined until the year 2140, meaning there's quite a bit of time to get in on the action if you're an investor.

Chapter 6
Modern Uses of Blockchain

While cryptocurrency is the buzz of the investment circle, blockchain technology is the real focus of many in the business and innovation circles who are starting to tap its potential as a revolutionary player in the way records are kept, data is guarded, and business takes place. Here are some use case studies of companies around the world who have already taken the plunge with this next-generation technology.

Mata Capital

Mata Capital is a French company that specializes in real estate fund management. In its chosen industry, there are three current difficulties that companies are facing. The first is that investors have limited access to secondary markets. This makes it tougher for them to trade assets, even when this strategy is suggested for portfolio allocation. The second is that there are large administration costs for small investment projects and registration activities, which results in investors being stuck with a high floor when it comes to investment subscription accounts. The third difficulty is that it is both costly and difficult to create funds, distribute assets, and perform registry maintenance. Prior to 2019, Mata Capital was performing all these registration processes on paper, which weighed and slowed things down even more.

The company decided to invest in blockchain technology that year to keep up with the times and become as efficient as possible with the maintenance of its investor registry and the distribution of its fund shares.

The first step for Mata was defining who was allowed to invest, what the shares owned represented, and what the rules were for performing transactions. All of these are necessary steps for investing in the building of a hotel property in compliance with particular regulatory requirements.

Teaming with an Ethereum-based company, Mata created smart contracts that encompassed validating investor Know-Your-Customer (KYC) forms, describe the asset in question, define the requirements for compliance specific to the country or region where the asset will be located, and give accurate fund shares to each verified investor.

By invoking the potential investors to create an account, fill out the KYC form, and upload other required documents to the blockchain platform, Mata was significantly reducing the "busy work" it would normally take on in this sort of process. The eligible investors were quickly put into one category, which automatically validated their credentials inside the platform; the rest were moved outside of it and kept on file for potential further investment opportunities.

With all the approved investors' information already sorted and verified, those eligible could also make entries about how many shares they would want to purchase, the type of shares they wanted, and even pay for them via a wire transfer all done inside a blockchain environment with no room for errors or data leaks. It also allowed Mata to not transfer the shares until payment was validated, after which time a certificate signed with a private, encrypted key finished the transaction. Once it was formalized, investors received a link to the transaction on the existing Ethereum blockchain that is indelible and unchangeable.

By completely eliminating so many of the throwaway costs of doing things on paper in general, as well as the bureaucratic waste of time associated with collecting all information in a non-digital format, Mata Capital is able to reinvest those funds into exciting new pathways that give investors more avenues to join the party. By assigning tokens to its assets, it will be able to dramatically lower costs that are involved with user registration, onboarding, and subscription operation—these can all be done inside the online platform that is accessible from any Internet-capable device. By using the functionality of the blockchain, Mata believes it can cast a wider net at potential investors. Even more impressive, its long-term goal is to shrink the minimum investor subscription amount from its current price of €100,000 (about $120,000) all the way down to €1, allowing any investor to include it in a diverse portfolio. In 2019, Mata kicked off this first campaign for an 11-story hotel in its building on the outskirts of Paris with an issuance of €26 million.

Her Majesty's Land Registry (HMLR)

HMLR was first founded in 1862 to register ownership of land and property in England and Wales. It is a non-ministerial department of the UK government and reports to the Department for Business, Energy, and Industrial Strategy. Its duty is to register the ownership of property by guaranteeing title to registered estates and interests in lands. It does this by recording the ownership rights of freehold properties and leasehold properties where the lease has been granted for more than seven years. As of the current date, there are more than 25 million ownership titles in HMLR with a combined value of about $8.7 trillion. With its history dating back close to 160 years, there are obviously some catch-up opportunities for HMLR, which led to its interest in blockchain.

Different issues with HMLR's current system include:

- Poor transparency, which is dangerous in today's environment.
- Secondary markets that have become isolated due to their reliance on processing by hand.
- Disjointed processes and parties that must all coalesce to carry out a single transaction.
- High minimum amounts required to invest, which means a smaller number of investors, unpredictable price swings when finding matches between buyers and sellers, and expensive processes throughout.
- Expensive maintenance of the investor registry, which is continuously behind the latest level of technology.

HMLR combined with a blockchain platform to create a digital token that would represent the ownership of a property. The owner of each property could decide how many tokens/shares they would offer for a virtual property as well as the price of said property. This worked just like a real property equivalent. The tokens, called "Title Tokens", would be offered in a digital asset marketplace and have an 8-part process to completion. The breakdown went like this:

1. Property owners gain Title Tokens for shares of an owned property. The tokens are digital copies of a title deed.

2. Property owners use a digital wallet that verifies their identity and connects them to an Ethereum-powered blockchain.
3. HMLR automatically transfers the Title Token to the owner's wallet once the verification process is complete.
4. Each property owner can then create security tokens that are linked to their new Title Tokens.
5. The owner decides the number of security tokens, the price of said tokens, the total amount being offered, and any other specifications relevant to the sale of these tokens.
6. Owners verify the details, then use a digital marketplace to manage and trade their tokens.
7. Investors can use the same marketplace to view available security token offerings, perform asset trading, manage property portfolios, and access asset data sourced by HMLR.
8. Industry regulators can access token data such as pricing in real time or capitalization, as well as on-chain activities including when trades take place and for how much.

When all of this was put in place, the blockchain technology advancement allowed HMLR to save on costs, reduce time spent on verification, increase customization of products, broaden access to investors who don't have the resources to buy an entire property; and build proof of evidence for the trading of fractional property assets, which opens a very narrow market wide to all sorts of potential investors. With such a high-stakes endeavor as real estate, the Ethereum blockchain is a magnificent source of comfort and security for owners and investors.

Komgo

Komgo is the first blockchain-based platform for trading commodities in a secure environment. It has places for banks, carriers, traders, and other parties to make secure, digital transitions that simplify the typical operations and documentation needed to make things turn. It launched at the end of 2018, going into production just four months after becoming incorporated and issuing its first letter of credit the next day; the first time that has happened on a blockchain platform for the commodity trade finance industry. About six months later, it unveiled features for standby letters of credit and receivable discounts.

In August 2019, ING completed its first commodity translation on Komgo, an oil deal with a Letter of Credit on behalf of Mercuria Energy Trading SA. The next month, Lloyds bank was the first UK bank to join the platform and that October, Komgo had surpassed $700 million of financing. The platform is now backed by 15 of the largest banks, trading companies, and oil mammoths in the world.

The blockchain-powered platform was created to shore up some of the biggest problems in the world of trading commodities. Those typically include:

- Miscommunication
- Language barriers
- Security flaws
- Potential for fraud
- Manual tasks that take lots of time and have the potential for human errors
- Transaction fees
- Bad invoices
- Delayed payments

Clearly a better technology could have an immense effect on such a business model. Bad processes and regulation failures contribute to the global trade finance supply/demand gap of a whopping $1.5 trillion. Komgo has a fine seat at the table, with its network based on JPMorgan's Quorum. It has its own proprietary document transit system known as Kite that allows for secure transfers without exposing any content anywhere along Komgo's chain. Ledger technology is at play here to digitize all documents, decrease fraud, and make the process as efficient as possible.

Transparency is up for the entire process while the blockchain architecture stresses private peer-to-peer transactions. This ensures someone private contract negotiations are not broadcast to the entire chain. There are a host of different parties that can get authorized on the platform, including commodity traders, energy corporations, inspection companies, and banks. With commodity training there is obviously a slew of regulation material that must be met. This can be a catastrophic waste of funds, resources, and time when done manually and on paper, so Komgo has enabled an enterprise blockchain to speed things along.

This starts with tamper-proof Know your Customer (KYC records that specifically meet international Anti-Money Laundering (AML regulations. The shared ledger gives tremendous access to strong, solid information for any of the platform's users, and ensures private data is only exchanged with correct verification and permission.

By the end of a few months, Komgo had provided an increase in cash flow between 30-40% thanks to its ability to streamline operations. In the long haul, Komgo estimates being able to reduce operational costs across the entire industry by 20-50%.

A second strength is putting everyone across the globe on the same software platform. This really breaks down language barriers and makes for far more simple procedures when it comes to communication and operations. Security is of course a major factor as well. Data cannot be altered, changed, or lost thanks to the blockchain-based software in play. Only certain participants can view some of the documentation, and attempts to change anything will be met with resistance and prosecution.

As of the time of writing, banks that have joined forces with Komgo include ABN-AMRO, BNP Paribas, Credit Agricole, Citi, Gunvor, ING, Koch Supply & Trading, Macquarie, Mercurial, MUFG Bank, Natixis, Rabobank, SGS, Shell, and Societe Generale.

August Debouzy

A leading French law firm, August Debouzy, uses its legal expertise to advise clients on the proper issuance of financial instruments, such as bonds, fund shares, and equities. Its mission in expanding into the realm of blockchain is to do so while slicing the costs and the complications of using a wide range of intermediaries and distributors. Doing this all while staying in compliance is never a difficult task. August Debouzy has been in business since 1995 and has 150 lawyers at work along with 30 partners focused on French and EU law.

The law firm was interested in the creation of Security Token Offerings (STOs which are gaining traction as a source of financing of investments for companies and asset managers. These tokens can make the investment process easier and more efficient for both investors and those issuing the investments. Costs can be lowered dramatically with digitization of assets, since blockchain can enable a lot of automation, streamlining of back-office processes like accounting, and cut out certain intermediary functionality that can all take place on the digital platform secured by blockchain. When used correctly, such things as clearing, voting proxies, and settlements can all be done digitally, resulting in a huge savings of time, resources, and manpower. The STOs are pre-coded so they can only be transferred if specific conditions have been met, greatly driving down the possibility of fraud or misuse.

Project i2i:

i2i stands for three things—Island-to-Island, Institution-to-Institution, and Individual-to-Individual. Those islands are the Philippines, with a population of more than 100 million people and an emerging economy. Despite all that, more than 70 million Filipinos are unbanked and have very little access to either global or domestic financial systems. A lot of these people work overseas, meaning a lot of the country's GDP is drawn from international remittances. Tackling the problem head on is UnionBank of the Philippines, partnering with such powerhouses as Microsoft Azure and Amazon AWS to create an inter-rural bank payment platform using Ethereum. 70% of people in the country do not have a checking or savings account and live on less than $2 per day. UnionBank tried to partner with 476 local banks, but most of them are not part of money transfer networks or electronic banking services. Instead they chose a blockchain partnership with seven local banks to create a decentralized real-time bank payment platform to help remote banks integrate on one standard system. In 2019, the system launched partnerships with 130 rural banks. The central bank of the government has signed off on it and Project i2i now operates the country's first Ethereum-based payment network. Its latest plan is to include international fund transfers for individuals, which would significantly reduce the wait time for funds from relatives working overseas as well as reduce the fees involved in getting those funds where they are needed most.

BurstIQ

Based in Colorado, BurstIQ is a platform that creates "health wallets" that manage data about a patient's health and wellness using both blockchain and the increasingly popular analysis of big data by virtue of AI. These wallets allow healthcare professionals to see high-level information about patients' medical records and wellness plans, but not any identifying personal information. They can then buy, sell or trade patient data for scientific studies, or for use in learning about specific conditions such as a kind of cancer or an addiction. BurstIQ's main focus is the opioid crisis, which is quite prevalent in Colorado and obviously has people hesitant to take part in studies because of the damage it could do to them personally or professionally. BurstIQ is using its blockchain technology to help develop treatment plans, services from doctors and other programs to reduce dependency on opioids. The company was founded in 2015 with a stated mission of "enabling a predictive, preventative, and personal era of health." The security and "lock and key" technology of blockchain ensures that no records are released accidentally, and no personal information inside those records can be leaked. It uses a private, permission-based data network to allow organizations to connect, share data, and collaborate on health solutions. This includes pharmaceutical and life science companies, along with government agencies and health systems. In 2021, BurstIQ was named the third-best blockchain company in Colorado.

Hurricane Disaster Relief

In August 2017 Hurricane Harvey hit Texas and Louisiana as a Category 4 hurricane, doing $125 billion of damage and causing more than 100 deaths. Although most hurricanes in the Gulf Coast region are known for their high winds, this one was different. It did not continue moving inland because of another pressure system holding it in place, and instead dumped record-setting amounts of rain on Southeast Texas. Many places in the Houston metropolitan area recorded more than 30 inches of rain, with a maximum of 60 inches deep. In East Texas, a representative of the Tyler County Emergency Management department issued a statement to residents choosing to remain behind and face the flooding: "Anyone who chooses not to evacuate cannot expect to be rescued and should write their social security numbers in permanent marker on their arm so their bodies can be identified. The loss of life and property is certain. GET OUT OR DIE!" As you can expect, the aftermath of this tragedy pushed the efforts of government agencies, relief funds, insurance companies, and victims to the limit. Endless paperwork to fill out was difficult for residents who no longer had a home to live in, much less a mailbox to get the forms delivered to. The whole process —known as disaster management—needed relief, and got it from IBM, which was contacted by the Speaker of the Texas House of Representatives to help manage the situation by making it easier to keep track of victim data without it getting lost, warped or misplaced. It allowed the Texas government —both state and local—to streamline processes and keep the ball rolling through multiple agencies and a blend of private and public channels to get people's insurance claims filed and help them regain their footing more quickly.

Mediachain

The entertainment industry has embraced new technology like few others in the past 20 years. Mediachain works in the music business and is an advocate for musicians and artists to get them their royalty checks on time and paid in full, something that has notoriously been a problem over the years. Mediachain uses a decentralized, transparent contract which allows all parties to see there are no microscopic details or 'read between the lines' issues involved. By using content addressing, Mediachain ensures that its data is tamper-proof and has no central point of control, meaning the media company has no more control of a contract than the artist. Those artists have specific cryptography attached to their identities to ensure nothing is changed without their knowledge. Mediachain is powered by Ethereum and was purchased by Spotify in 2017.

Royal Dutch Shell

This long-time industry giant has developed an energy blockchain platform in concert with Sinochem Technologies and the Macquarie Group. The platform is for trade and settlement of oil and gas with the idea of reducing inefficiencies that occur when trading and settling commodities across oceans and languages. Blockchain also allows for an increase in transparency for all parties as well as greater transparency and much less risk of fraud thanks to the cryptographic nature of security in blockchain. Known as the Vakt platform, the blockchain technology houses multiple oil companies, including the aforementioned Shell, BP, and Norway's Equinor. Three trading companies—Guvnor, Koch Supply and Trading, and Gunvor, are also involved.

Walmart

When you're a corporation as big as Walmart—11.443 stores in 26 countries and total assets exceeding $252.5 billion—you need to be on top of your supply chain lest a disaster strike that damages your public image. In the fall of 2020, an e.coli virus outbreak in Romaine lettuce was centered around Walmart with cases reported in six different states—Virginia, Pennsylvania, Ohio, Michigan, Illinois and California. With such a vast supply chain and so many outlets, Walmart and its subsidiary, Sam's Club, sent letters to suppliers announcing the recall. Since then, the company has worked to install blockchain technology along its supply chain to be able to trace any individual food product all the way back to the farm. Doing so will establish for Walmart what many advocates of food safety and visibility have been preaching for years: end-to-end traceability and accountability from farm to table. Blockchain tech allows this to be a real-time activity that makes every step of the process open to ensure supplier accountability. It will give Walmart the ability to source where the bad lettuce came from and either work with that supplier to root out the problem, or remove that supplier altogether. According to Walmart's corporate website, having an in-place blockchain system could allow employees to reduce the time to trace contaminated food down from about 7 days to as little as 2.2 seconds.

State of West Virginia

In 2018, the state of West Virginia partnered with a blockchain app company known as Voatz (votes) to run a successful test in two counties during the US midterm election primaries. Voters from West Virginia currently living overseas would typically vote via mail-in ballots, but instead used the app to punch their choices. These voters were mostly those serving overseas in the military or as members of the Peace Corps.

Chapter 7
Rise of the Cryptocurrencies

As we have touched on many times throughout this book, Bitcoin was the first cryptocurrency even before the term "cryptocurrency" had been defined. As such, it has become the fabric of society when it comes to what most people think of when they hear the term. However, there have been many more types of cryptocurrencies come into existence in the 13 years since Nakamoto first introduced the idea. In this chapter we will chart not only the history of Bitcoin, but of several other pivotal cryptocurrencies that have made an impact on the market overall.

Bitcoin

As detailed in Chapter 1, Bitcoin first went live in the early days of 2009, with Hal Finney being the first person to ever be on the receiving end of a bitcoin transaction. A year later, Bitcoin celebrated its first commercial transaction when a programmer named Laszlo Hanyecz bought two pizzas for 10,000 bitcoins. Nakamoto vanished as mysteriously as he had appeared in 2010, mining approximately 1 million bitcoins and giving control of both the network alert key and the code repository to a man named Gavin Andresen. Andresen was developing products for Bitcoin in 2010 and was named its lead developer by Nakamoto, developing client software for the network that is now renamed Bitcoin Core. In 2016, he claimed that an Australian programmer named Craig Wright was the real identity of Nakamoto. Wright has attempted to augment these claims but most of the crypto community and the media that follows such things does not believe him.

Before Bitcoin really hit the mainstream, it was very nearly destroyed by a rogue hacker in August 2010. The hacker, never named, found an exploit in the code for checking transactions. If outputs were so large that they overflowed when added together, the code for checking the transactions stopped working. At the time there was a limited supply of 21 million Bitcoin in existence. The hacker was able to exploit the code to create 184.467 billion bitcoins all at once in what has come to be known as the Value Overflow

Incident. Fortunately, Nakamoto and Andresen were on the case and were able to flip the switch the other way. They created a code fix within five hours that was quickly released. Not only did it remove the 184 billion bitcoins but it fixed the exploit so it would not happen again.

It was the first attempted hack of Bitcoin but it unfortunately would not be the last, a fact that kept the cryptocurrency from gaining legroom and legitimacy for several years across America and worldwide markets. The open-source code also spawned the emergence of other coins, which might have been viewed as a negative to some, but suggested that there was enough legitimacy at play to create a competitive market, something that investors took particular notice of. In 2011, nonprofits like WikiLeaks and The Electronic Frontier Foundation began taking donations in the form of bitcoins. Otherwise, 2011 was not a year to remember for Bitcoin. In 2010, US programmer Jed McCaleb had created a cryptocurrency platform called Mt. Gox that became the hub for most Bitcoin trades over the next few years. In March 2011, it had its first black eye at the fragile age of just eight months. While undergoing a change in owners, the site was hacked and 80,000 bitcoins were stolen. Craig Wright, who falsely claimed to be Nakamoto, said the account the coins were stolen from was his.

The next attack on Bitcoin was even more coordinated. It began on June 13, 2011, when a hacker infiltrated the computer of a member of the Bitcoin mining pool called Slush Pool, stealing 25,000 bitcoins. But his 'work' was not done there. He sent the stolen coins to Mt. Gox and sold them for $480,000 in a clean get-away. Six days later, Mt. Gox suffered another hit when owner Jed McCaleb administration account was hacked. The person invading it knew exactly what they were doing, using artificial methods to drop the price of a bitcoin from $17 down to a single penny. The hacker then bought 2,000 bitcoins at the miniscule price and promptly transferred them out of the exchange before the error was noticed or fixed. This was just part of a large hack that ultimately spelled doom for Mt. Gox. When the theft was taking place in June 2011, it is believed that hackers also gained access to the site's private key and the unencrypted version of its wallet.dat file, which allowed them access to virtually every account on the system. Between June 2011 and February 2014, the hacks were able to steal about 744,000 coins owned by users and another 100,000 owned by Mt. Gox, as well as $27 million in cash from Mt. Gox, by siphoning them off in small, virtually unnoticeable amounts. While the website was able to find some missing coins, it still was not able to stay in business and had to file for bankruptcy. The fiasco was so widespread that it created a new word in the industry, "goxxed" which means waking up to find out your investment is gone, and you should have known better. Almost as rough as the hacks was the fact that the only sites using bitcoin for financial transactions in those early days were black markets on the Dark Web. At the beginning of 2011, the price of a single bitcoin was a mere $0.30, but by the end of the year it rose to $5.27 per coin, an increase of more than 1,657%. The next two years saw a price rollercoaster that would ebb and flow at random. It reached $16.41 by August of 2012, only to drop 57% just three days later.

The currency began gaining steam in 2012 when it made its first televised appearance on the CBS drama series "The Good Wife". Popular TV financial commentator Jim Cramer appeared as himself in a courtroom scene where he didn't think Bitcoin was a real currency. Nine months later, Andresen and several other members of the early Bitcoin crowd launched the Bitcoin Foundation with the motivation to "accelerate the global growth of Bitcoin through standardization, protection, and promotion of the open-source goal." It appeared as if the powers that be at Bitcoin had realized that it would never gain true legitimacy without a guiding force, no matter how novel and revolutionary its technology and concept were. The commitment to a level of professionalism and process worked wonders for Bitcoin. A month later, BitPay, the app that was developed to allow merchants to accept bitcoin as payment, had more than 1,000 stores using its service. By November 2012, WordPress, the globally known website building service, became the first really well-known name to start accepting bitcoins as payment for its products and services. The strides kept coming in 2013 with the website Internet Archive not only taking payments in bitcoin, but offering it to their employees as a way to receive some of their salaries in the cryptocurrency This growth was temporarily interrupted by a technical error that caused two different blockchains to appear, causing a temporary sell-off, and a 23% price tip to $37 before it was fixed.

During that same time frame, the US government took its first official action about cryptocurrency, classifying people who mine it as Money Service Businesses and noting that they might be tasked with registration or other legal obligations in the future. The price moved past $100 for the first time, then up to $266 by April. Bitcoin spilled outside the American borders thanks to a light shined on it in Kenya, linking the cryptocurrency to that country's mobile payments system known as M-Pesa. In November 2013, China's BTC China exchange moved past Mt. Gox and the European-originated Bitstamp to become the largest by volume trading platform of bitcoin in the world. Ironically about a month later, China's government banned its own country's banks and other financial services from accepting bitcoin, causing the price to drop. But it rebounded just as quickly and rose to $770/coin by January 1, 2014.

While it looked like Bitcoin was going to be on the rise for a while, investor sentiment quickly reversed. The cryptocurrency was under more and more of a spotlight from the mainstream media and economic traditionalists were seeking to cast it out as a fake currency and an investment into a product that had no real value or meaning. The harsh limelight caused a selling frenzy to start the year and within 365 days, it closed at $320.19, having dropped 140% over the course of the year. The next two years were volatile and seemingly arbitrary. Every time the cryptocurrencies would shoot up, something would bring them back down.

In 2015, the 0.10 launch of the software came in February. It improved a number of features, including a library that showed programmers how to quickly access the rules of consensus on the network. With each new release, Bitcoin made itself more and more accessible to the general public, driving up interest in it and pushing its value higher and higher. By February of 2017, the price of a single bitcoin leapt from $970 up to $1,200, eventually settling at $1,179.97 by month's end. By then, the technology for Bitcoin also included Bitcoin Core, another security measure to keep things copasetic inside the trading platform.

The increase in value of bitcoins brought with it another round of cybercrime. This time it was Hong Kong's Bitfinex exchange being hit in August 2016. A security breach saw just short of 120 bitcoins valued at $72 million stolen. It was a baffling attack given that Bitfinex had significant security with a multi-signature wallet system using three keys. The customers who lost their money were specifically upset because the system had no sort of flagging system to review such a massive sized order. Two years later the US government had recovered about 27 of the missing coins, but the rest was still missing. The rest of the coins remained unmoved, perhaps due to stricter laws in place. In June 2019, just a few weeks after some of the coins were finally moved, Israeli cyber police arrested brothers Eli and Assaf Gigi who had perpetrated the crime when Eli was 28 and Assaf just 18.

By the middle of 2017, Bitcoin was ready for its next quantum leap forward when the SegWit software upgrade was approved with the intent of improving scalability. The market responded and prices soared from $998 at the start of the year to a stunning $13,412 per coin at the start of 2018. The integration was not well received by all, and some supporters split off to form Bitcoin Cash that August to keep their own version and vision of the software intact. The volatility would continue to be one of Bitcoin's main weaknesses in the years to come as China out and out banned the use of it completely in February 2018. This caused another large shift in the price. After reaching an all-time high of $19,783 on December 27, 2017, it plummeted to $6,914 on February 5, 2018—a drop of 186% in just 40 days. More hacks and security exposures saw the price fall even farther to just $3,747 on January 1, 2019. This was largely the result of rampant hacks in 2018, with more than $761 million of cryptocurrencies stolen from various exchanges just in the first six months of 2019. But things turned around in September 2019 when the owner of the New York Stock Exchange, the International Exchange, announced it would create a new market called Bakkt to be run exclusively for Bitcoin futures. After YouTube had previously removed cryptocurrency and Bitcoin videos, they were restored in December 2019. The price finished 2019 at $7,571.

As the world struggled to make sense of the COVID-19 pandemic beginning in February and March of 2020, interest in cryptocurrency and Bitcoin in general soared. The exchange Kraken saw an 83% rise in new accounts the week of March 11 when countries around the world began shutting down much of their business and infrastructure. After being bought higher into the $10,000 range in February, it fell along with most other markets around the world down to below $4,000 on March 13. The dip was short-lived, however, as Bitcoin crested back up above $10,000 by May of 2020. In August, MicroStrategy announced it would invest $250 million in bitcoin as a treasury reserve asset, and the price rose to $13,781 by the end of September. The following month, Square put 1% of its assets, about $50 million in bitcoin, and in November, the biggest fish in the lake, PayPal, announced that its users could buy, sell, and hold bitcoin on its platform. The effect was instantaneous. The price per coin jumped nearly $10,000 to $29,001 to close November 2020 and rose above $35,000 to start 2021.

Ethereum

Ethereum is the second-largest cryptocurrency behind Bitcoin in terms of market share. Ethereum was founded on the power of its blockchain, which is the most-used of its kind in the world. While Bitcoin's value lies more in the currency and the ability to use if as an alternative way to store and trade, Ethereum's founder, Vitalik Buterin, wrote in a white paper that blockchain technology could benefit profoundly from applications beyond financial and that attaching real-world assets to it could be possible with the development of a new scripting language. Buterin is as much a marvel as the mysterious Nakamoto in that he co-founded Bitcoin Magazine in 2011 when he was all of 17 years old. A native of Russia, Buterin moved to Canada when he was six with his parents and immediately was recognized as a gifted and talented student. After one year of college, he dropped out when he won a grant for $100,000 from the Thiel Fellowship—run by noted venture capitalist Peter Thiel—who has been a notable investor in several 21st century paradigm shifters including PayPal and Facebook. Buterin unveiled Ethereum at the 2014 North American Bitcoin Conference. Buterin's initial plan saw it as a non-profit company. During beta testing, Buterin offered a 'bounty' of 25,000 Ether—the name of the currency—for anyone who could find bugs in the blockchain programming before release.

Ether is the cryptocurrency rewarded by miners doing the proof-of-work that allows blocks to be added to the blockchain. It is traded on the stock market under the name ETH and there are more than 110 million Ether in circulation as of 2020. Transaction fees can only be paid in Ether on the platform. There are several key differences between Bitcoin and Ethereum, the most fundamental one being that Bitcoin is a form of digital money while Ethereum is a platform for smart contracts that leverages blockchain technology. Ethereum can be used to create other coins or as a safehouse for other types of valuables according to the wishes of the users. While Bitcoin transaction fees are generated by the size of the transaction, those in Ethereum take several factors to create a term called "gas' which incorporates storage requirements, bandwidth used, and the complexity of the proof-of-work computations necessary to validate the transaction. To date, the blockchain technology language of Ethereum has been used for crowdfunding, including the initial coin offerings (ICOs) of other cryptocurrency, for gambling, for prediction markets, for video games, for decentralized finance, and for decentralized exchanges. The software has been used in testing of real-life applications by the likes of Barclays, Credit Suisse, Amazon, Deloitte, JPMorgan Chase, IBM, and Microsoft.

ETH debuted on the stock market at a mere $1.35 per coin back in August 2015 and immediately fell by 45% by the end of the month. It would not break even $1 per coin again until the end of January 2016 when it closed the month at $2.31. While Bitcoin began moving into the hundreds and the thousands of dollars per coin, Ethereum was in its immense shadows, finally gaining some traction in March of 2017 when it rose from $15.85 at the beginning of the month to $50.04 at the end. The price didn't stop there, not by a long shot. It hit $79 at the end of March 2017 then catapulted up to $230.67 at the end of April. After a slight lull in the summertime, the price kept climbing and hit $756.73 by the end of 2017, a stunning 10,000% increase.

A lot of the rise came from the production of ERC-20 tokens which debuted that year. ERC-20 tokens were used by many other companies to launch their own ICOs. They would use the Ethereum platform to produce fungible tokens, which means they are interchangeable. As a bonus to Ethereum, fees used to send ERC-20 tokens must be paid with Ether.

In January 2018, Ether became the second cryptocurrency after Bitcoin to exceed the price of $1,000 per coin. It peaked at $1,432.88, but was followed by an immediate downturn that saw the price plummet as low as the number of ICOs dropped significantly. In 2017, there were 875 ICOs that went through Ethereum, generating $6.2 billion in US funding, almost all of that passing through Ethereum.

The price bottomed out at a low of $82.83 per coin in December 2018 before moving back up to $133 by the end of the year. Its build back up was more graduated in 2019 as its blockchain technology got more of a book and the rush of ICOs leveled out. In the back half of 2020 it began to climb steadily and reached 737.80 at year's end. Ethereum started 2021 with a sharp climb up the price charts thanks to its focus on DeFi tokens (decentralized finance tokens which run on blockchains and recreate traditional banking and finance services without the third party. Most of the DeFi tokens in existence are running on Ethereum blockchains, giving the company a significant boost. In the first three weeks of 2021, Ethereum's price rose from $737.71 to as high as $1,382.27, busting its previous all-time high from February 2018.

Litecoin

If the name reminds you of Bitcoin, it is purposely done so. The Litecoin was an early variation of the Bitcoin, one of the first of a group of altcoins that began filling the market late in 2011. Like Bitcoin it is a peer-to-peer cryptocurrency and has open-source software. It was created by Charlie Lee, at the time a Google employee, who went on to become the Engineering Director of Coinbase. In October 2011, the Litecoin network went into effect as the result of a source-code fork that was Lee's invention. In blockchain parlance, a fork happens when different parties don't agree on how a blockchain should go forward. It can also be thought of as a change in protocol. There are two types of forks: hard and soft. A hard fork involves a rule change that invokes a permanent split in the blockchain. This happens because the change in the software that validates additions to the blockchain will see those blocks added under the new parameters be listed as invalid, thus creating a second, "new" chain. A soft fork describes a scenario in which the old nodes don't follow a rule that the new nodes subscribe to, which makes the old nodes continue to accept data deemed invalid by the newer nodes. It can make the blockchain appear out of sync, but does not involve the formation of a new block.

Litecoin took a source code fork from Bitcoin to decrease the amount of time a new block generation took, increased the maximum number of coins, and used a different hashing algorithm. The block processing time is just 2.5 minutes for Litecoin compared to 10 minutes for Bitcoin. The two currencies were still closely tied in the early days after the fork, but have diverged more and more as time has gone on. Litecoin's price never exceeded $10 until March 2017 when it began a rapid climb from $6.65 at the start of that month up to $232 by the end of the year. The slow transaction speed of Bitcoin was cited as a reason, as was the idea of diversification being a sound investment strategy for those just getting into the market as it heated up. With Litecoin's many similarities to the by then proven Bitcoin, it made sense for it to attract a lot of attention.

That first peak lasted for a couple of months before the cryptocurrency slid back down diving to a low mark of $22.82 near the end of December 2018. It has crossed the $100 threshold twice since then, touching $146.43 in May 2019 and rising to $185.78 in early January 2021, climbing almost $100 in the first month of the new year It has seen an inverse relationship with the US dollar—rising when the dollar is weak, indicating that people don't trust the world's most powerful currency and falling when the dollar is strong, such as when currencies like China's fall on news that the world's biggest nation is struggling with another outbreak of COVID-19.

Ripple

Ripple got its start in the US in 2012 and like Ethereum seeks to differentiate itself from Bitcoin by having a fundamental shift as its base. It is also like Ethereum because it was conceived in part by Ethereum founder Jed McCaleb, who built it along with Arthur Britto, David Schwartz, and Ryan Fugger. McCaleb did not see eye to eye with the other founders on the direction of the project and left early on to start Ethereum. Ripple's cryptocurrency goes by the designation XRP. The company describes itself as a distributed open source protocol that allows for any sort of "secure, instant, and nearly free global financial transactions of any size with no chargebacks." Ripple claims it can handle any sort of transaction and storage of any type of currency or units of value, ranging from cryptocurrency, fiat (hard) currency, stocks and other commodities, along with reward-type incentives such as mobile device minutes or data allowances, or frequent-flier miles. Ripple saw instant interest from banks curious about using its blockchain solutions as a payment system. By 2018, the cryptocurrency platform had signed up more than 100 banks to its service, but most of them were only using its XCurrent messenger technology and not the cryptocurrency aspect of the company because of the inherent volatility issues that all cryptocurrency has suffered from since inception.

The basis of Ripple is a common shard ledger which is a database storing information about all current Ripple accounts. There are independent servers powering Ripple's transactions which can be from anyone in the world. Ripple pushes on Bitcoin's dominance by offering the validation of its accounts, balances, and payment notifications in a near real-time environment. Ripple has been successful enough to gain the attention of the Society for Worldwide Interbank Financial Telecommunication (SWIFT) which has a virtual monopoly on this sort of transaction. If you have ever used your bank to transfer funds from someone overseas, you have likely been required to provide a SWIFT code to make it legitimate. In December 2014, Ripple started working with Earthport to use its software in the company's payment services system, the first network to work with Ripple. It has not been all bright and sunny for the company, however. In 2018 a class-action lawsuit against the organization claimed it had raised hundreds of millions of dollars in sales of its XRP tokens that were unregistered. It was labeled a "never-ending initial coin offering."

In late December of 2020, the United States Security and Exchange Commission (SEC) announced an investigation of Ripple, CEO Brad Garlinghouse, and co-founder Chris Larsen for selling XRP as an unregistered security. The SEC says XRP is not a commodity but a security because it is generated and distributed solely by Ripple Labs and that it is not being adopted by financial institutions despite that being its stated purpose. The accusation further states that Ripple brass has sold some 14.6 billion

XRP coins to a profit of $1.38 billion solely to fund its endeavors and as a profit for the CEO and C-suite executives. Ripple defended itself against these allegations, but in the final few days of 2020, XRP was delisted from Coinbase and an investor filed a class-action lawsuit against Coinbase about the same complaint that the SEC had made.

Tether

As far back as January 2012, a whitepaper was published suggesting that other currencies could be built on top of Bitcoin's open-source protocol. The author of that paper was J.R. Willett, who created the Mastercoin Foundation, which was the foundation for Tether. A second generation of it, known as Realcoin, started in July 2014 in Santa Monica, California. It was renamed Tether in November 2014 with the idea of three currencies: USTether (US+) for the US dollar, EuroTether (EU+) for euros and YenTether (JP+) for Japanese yen. The ownership declared that all the tokens would be backed 100% by their original currencies and could be redeemed at any time without any consequences of exchange rate. In January 2015, Bitfinex inaugurated Tether into its platform but within two years there was controversy as it seemed that the two independent companies were working together to set up Tether Holdings Limited in the British Virgin Islands. When pressed, it was revealed that Jan Ludovicus van der Velde was the CEO of both companies. This was only the tip of the iceberg for questionable behavior by Tether and its owners. In April 2017, the company announced that its previous process of sending US dollar transactions through Taiwanese banks had been blocked. It then announced it would use Ethereum's ERC20 tokens for US dollars and euros. In April 2019, the attorney general of New York State filed a suit accusing Bitfinex of using Tether's substantial reserves to cover up its own loss of some $850 million. Bitfinex had not been able to maintain a stable relationship with a normal financial institute and was instead using Tether to launder its money, and none of the investors of either company had ever been made aware of the arrangement. This came on the heels of a 2017 controversy in which Tether could not make good on its claim to allow users to withdraw funds into US dollars at any time. In November 2017, about $31 million of US+ tokens were stolen from Tether. The company suspended trading and took time to perform a hard fork to roll out new software to make up for the security breach, but the funds were never found or returned to their owners. In March 2019, it stopped claiming that its token was backed by the US dollar and changed the connection to loans from its affiliate companies.

Altcoins

Altcoins are a catch-all phrase for any token, digital asset, or form of cryptocurrency that is not defined as a bitcoin. Bitcoin is definitely the patriarch of this niche, but there are many different forms of altcoins that do many other things. All the companies mentioned in this chapter other than Bitcoin itself are examples of altcoins. The word is clearly a combination of alternative and coin and today there are more than 5,000 of these altcoins created across the world. They come in many different categories based on what their functionality is, including stablecoins, security tokens, utility tokens, and mining-based cryptocurrencies. As of February 2020, more than 34% of the total cryptocurrency market was made up of altcoins. Like Bitcoin, most altcoins work on a peer-to-peer network. Mining-based altcoins are the most like Bitcoin because they are generated by people's computers doing the computations necessary to ensure the validity of the transactions. Stablecoins are founded on the purpose of reducing volatility in the cryptocurrency realm. Tether attempted to be one of those but with mixed results. Many others seek to be backed by the US dollar, the euro, or the gold standard.

Security tokens represent a specific business and are usually offered during an ICO. They are the closest thing in the market to a traditional stock offering, with some even offering dividends to holders.

Utility tokens also are often born of ICOs, and give the holder a claim on a future service. An example of this is the Filecoin, which is a marker that enables the holder to have a certain amount of decentralized file storage space.

Diem (Libra)

Other than Bitcoin and Ethereum, the cryptocurrency/blockchain project that has received the most buzz in the past few years is Diem, formerly known as

Libra. Why is that significant? Two reasons: 1) It hasn't even come out yet as of the publishing of this book, and 2) It's being created by Facebook. The project has been in the works since at least 2017 when Morgan Beller, formerly with Medium, started the project. Beller has since left Facebook to take a position with venture capital firm NFX. David A. Marcus, vice-president in charge of Facebook Messenger, moved to the newly-created blockchain division in May 2018, and within a few days the rumors were out that Facebook was planning a cryptocurrency. By the following February, the ranks of engineers working on the project had surpassed 50. The cryptocurrency was announced during a particularly rough year for Facebook. In March of that year, Brenton Harrison Tarrant, a 28-year-old Australian man, had used Facebook's live stream feature to broadcast himself as he drove to a mosque in New Zealand and opened fire with automatic weapons on the worshippers gathered inside. He live streamed for 17 minutes and it took Facebook roughly 30 minutes to take the footage down, by which time it had been copied more than 1.6 million times. In November 2019, the banking data of more than 29,000 Facebook employees was stolen from the car of one of its payroll employees. Said data was being stored on hard drives without encryptions and contained such information as employee names, partial social security numbers, salaries, bank account numbers, and bonuses. Facebook was unaware of the theft for three days and did not inform employees of the theft for nearly a month.

These events came on the heels of Zuckerberg's testimony in front of the US Senate Committee on Commerce, Science, and Transportation in April 2018 regarding how the company was using personal data. In March 2018, Facebook was found to have been duped by Cambridge Analytica which had gobbled up massive information on the profiles of millions of people. Facebook had not alerted users when the breach was discovered. Most of the data that was taken without consent was used for political advertising and it remains the largest leak in Facebook history. Cambridge Analytica sold the data on American voters to multiple political campaigns including those of Texas Senator Ted Cruz and current US President Donald Trump. The app was created in 2013 but the controversy was only revealed through the actions of Christopher Wylie, a former Cambridge Analytica employee, through a series of interviews with both *The Guardian* and *The New York*

Times. The day the articles were released in March 2018 saw Facebook's market valuation drop by $100 billion. Cambridge Analytica claimed it had "only" collected 30 million Facebook profiles while the articles set the number at 50 million. Facebook later confirmed it was actually north of 87 million people, nearly 71 million of them hailing from the United States. Only after the articles were published did Facebook send a message to potentially affected users, telling them that if they had given the app permission, it was possible that Cambridge Analytica had accessed their News Feeds, timelines, and even messages to other users. Just seven months later, Facebook was in hot water again when it admitted to a data breach that affected more than 50 million people as hackers were able to exploit a code weakness to view people's profiles in a privacy mode.

In June 2019, Facebook made the formal announcement that its cryptocurrency project, then called Libra, was underway with a release date some time in 2020. A month later, the company released another statement that the cryptocurrency would not launch anywhere in the world until it had met all regulatory concerns and had appropriate approval from US and other countries' government agencies.

While cryptocurrency aficionados might have been excited at the initial announcement, government agencies and banks had a distinctly opposite opinion. The official announcement came as French Finance Minister Bruno Le Maire was being interviewed on a national radio program. His immediate response was negative, with him saying Libra would require strong consumer protections and could not be a sovereign currency as it would disrupt established infrastructure around the world. He did not stop there, warning France's Parliament that he had strong concerns about Facebook in terms of privacy, the possibility of finance for terrorism, and money laundering— something that has plagued cryptocurrencies since their foundation.

While the Bank of England's governor Mark Carney stated he would keep an open mind on the possible new crypto, Germany's MEP Markus Ferber was the first to bring up the term "shadow bank" —a term often used to describe the likes of loan sharks. It more broadly refers to financial exchanges that are not banks. A bail bondsman would qualify under this terminology or even a pawn shop. Fellow German MEP Stefan Berger said in an interview that Libra would be a threat to the euro zone's economic stability as well as the democracies that encompass it, suggesting that the eurozone would be wise to develop its own Stablecoin as a more secure alternative. France's Le Maire followed up his initial criticisms in September 2019 by stating that France would not allow Libra in the EU at all, casting it as an economic threat to those nations' stability. Because of Facebook's well-known data mining of its users, the concern for a lack of privacy came from many sectors, including Japan, the US, and the EU. Facebook has said that its subsidiary, Novi Financial, will manage Libra for Facebook users, but it will not share account holders' information with Facebook without authorization from users.

In the United States, concern from the political and regulatory sectors came within hours of the initial announcement in 2019. Most dramatic and to the point of these was the response of Maxine Waters, the Chairperson of the United States House Committee on Financial Services. She asked Zuckerberg and Facebook to completely halt the development and launch of Libra with reasons of Facebook's string of recent scandals as well as the fact that the "cryptocurrency market currently lacks a clear regulatory framework." Of course, that might be the very reason Facebook is trying to launch its cryptocurrency in the near future—before such regulations are put in concrete and would affect the way it is created, instead of having to only bend to meet later-established criteria. Democrats from that House Committee sent an official letter to Facebook to cease development with lead concerns of monetary policy, trading, national security, and privacy, about as strong a request as a committee can send.

This was followed by a testimony by Jerome Powell, Chairman of the Federal Reserve, in front of the US Congress in July 2019. He reiterated the committee's concern about how Facebook would handle common financial issues including financial stability, consumer protection, and money laundering. Then-President Donald Trump, who even before becoming the US Commander in Chief in 2016 has rallied against breaking up Internet companies such as Facebook, Amazon, and Google which he views as monopolies, tweeted that "if Facebook and other companies want to become a bank, they must seek a new banking Charter and become subject to all

Banking Regulations."

US regulators went a step further, getting in contact from established payment companies such as Stripe, Mastercard, Visa, and PayPal, charging them to analyze how Libra would conform with their own anti-money laundering protection programs.

Marcus, Facebook's VP in charge of the project, had told the US Senate that the company would use the Swiss Federal Data Protection and Information Commissioner to oversee Libra's privacy policies. This turned into egg on the company's face later that year when the Swiss organization said it had never been contacted by anyone from Facebook.

Facebook faced more trouble over the registration of the terms "Libra," "LIBRA," and "Libra Association" in both the EU and the US, at least in part prompting the name change to Diem Association—Diem being the Latin word for "day" as in "Carpe diem".

The project has now been delayed and has no set release date. There are not a lot of available details, presumably because Facebook has been more close-fisted about its proprietary information since its initial announcement was met with so much official criticism. It is known that Diem will not use cryptocurrency mining and that only members of the so-called "Diem Association" will be able to process transactions inside the blockchain. Facebook hopes to move to a proof-of-stake system that does not require permissions in the first five years of its cryptocurrency, although the company's engineers admit that at their current level of technology, they do not have the capability to expand the scale, security, or stability of that system if it were to be used by any substantial number of Facebook users. The software source code is written in Rust and will be joined by a digital wallet as a standalone app that can be integrated through both Messenger and WhatsApp. Originally called Calibra, it has since had its name changed to Novi, but as of March 2021 had no release date.

Facebook has also announced plans for Move, its smart contract/custom transactions language. Its language syntax has yet to be released, although a whitepaper on its creation and use has been published.

In March 2021, another of the cryptocurrency's co-inventors, Kevin Weil, left the company, taking a job as president of Planet Labs.

Chapter 8
An Investor's Guide to Cryptocurrency

In a relatively short span of time, cryptocurrency has burst onto the investment scene and made waves, with people of all ages and backgrounds testing the waters.

The blockchain technology is appealing to many long-term investors for its potential use in other fields, such as the keeping of medical records. As more and more companies adapt to the blockchain, crypto companies that use it best will rise in value.

Short-term investors tend to ride the hype, so to speak; jumping in and out of different currencies as they come into play or spike on industry news.

It's easy to misinterpret cryptocurrency as a younger person's game. The technology and concept behind it are not the easiest to understand, but the same could be said for dot-com companies in the 1990s, or even the likes of Apple and IBM when personal computers arose in the late 1970s and early 1980s. While millennials do hold a lot of cryptocurrency—one survey pegs 39% of its holders to be between 25-34 years old—there are ample opportunities for Generation X and Baby Boomers to invest in crypto for their own goals and come away the better for it.

What are the motivations for each generation to invest in cryptocurrency and how many are doing it? Let's take a deeper dive into each age group and their investment portfolio.

Millennials: Cryptocurrency, in many ways, is scratching millennials right where they itch. The generation of Americans who have grown up with the Internet and smartphones as part of their lives from a young age are the most adept at understanding and trusting the technology sector. Cryptocurrency and blockchain are both at the forefront of that digital wave. A survey of cryptocurrency investors released in March 2018 found 22.7% of cryptocurrency holders to be in their 20s and an additional 19.3% in their 30s.

Millennials also have a healthy distrust of big banks. When the mortgage crisis of 2007-2010 occurred in the US, most millennials were in their teens or early 20s; highly impressionable times for a person to form opinions on a major part of the country's infrastructure. That same crisis likely dampened many millennials' interest in investing in the stock market. The Great Recession shredded the retirement funds and 401(k) plans of many millennials' parents. The challenge of investing in cryptocurrency for millennials resides in their availability of funds to invest. With Bitcoin now selling for the price of a new car per share, there aren't a lot of millennials able to get in on the highest-priced cryptocurrency. The smaller cryptos are harder to quantify in terms of what's real and what's just a passing fancy.

Generation Xers: Generation X has the unfortunate claim of having the most credit card debt out of the three targeted demographics. Paying off lots of debt means less money to invest for the short-term or long-term. Two different studies reveal that 50% of Gen Xers say they won't start saving for retirement until their credit card debt is paid off, and that 40% of them don't know how they're paying for retirement. With 15-20 years of work already in the rearview mirror, Generation Xers find themselves needing to hustle to make up for lost time and get their IRAs up to snuff. Cryptocurrency can be a great way to catch up in a hurry if the right investments are made at the right time. Bitcoin was priced right around $1,000 at the beginning of 2017 and is now above $30,000. Had a Gen Xer invested $5,000 during that early period, they would now have an additional $200,000. Even better, they can use self-directed IRAs to put crypto into a retirement account. Self-directed IRAs work just like regular ones, except that you are the director of the funds, not an investment firm. Anything from traditional stocks and bonds to precious metals to crypto to property can be placed in a self-directed IRA.

The key for Generation Xers, who by now are settled into the traditional family model of spouses, kids, minivans, and mortgage payments, is finding long-term investment opportunities that will consistently increase in value. This takes lots of research and smart decision-making, avoiding the knee-jerk reactions to cryptos that rise meteorically, only to quickly burn out.

Baby Boomers: Baby Boomers were hit the hardest by the Great Recession, with an average of 25% loss from the retirement accounts of those who had been on the job for 20 years. Many Boomers have spent the 10 years since taking more chances in an attempt to regain all those losses to reach retirement age with the finances they had been planning for prior to the recession. Trust is a big negative for Boomers with crypto. There's no safety net, buying it isn't that easy, and there aren't many ways to spend it that appeal to them, other than buying other cryptocurrencies. One survey finds less than 7% of crypto buyers are over the age of 55.

Another barrier for Boomers is the foreign concept of cryptocurrency. It's tough to invest dollars in something that you don't understand. But the same could be said about the rise of the digital superpowers like Amazon and Google. Companies with sound business plans are worth looking into, regardless of what they actually do.

Chapter 9
A Legal Guide to Cryptocurrency and Blockchain

From the outside looking in, cryptocurrency can be hard to define and even harder to quantify. Not surprisingly, that makes it a bit of a legal conundrum as well. This is to be expected given how revolutionary a financial device cryptocurrency is. Cryptocurrency might have gotten its start in the United States, and thus be beholden first and foremost to US laws, but it has spread like wildfire around the world, with individual countries having varied reactions to whether it should be legal or not, how it is classified, how it can be traded, what part of each government is responsible for its regulation, etc. This of course butts heads with the original intent and hope of cryptocurrency in general and Bitcoin specifically as a form of exchange that would exist outside of the parameters of governments and financial institutions. That might have been the original intent, but governments wouldn't be governments if they let systems that involve finances go completely unchecked.

As of the spring of 2021, US law defining and regulating cryptocurrency is all over the place. One thing remains a certainty, the US government does not consider cryptocurrency to be legal tender because it is not backed by the authority of a government or a central financial entity. That's good news for traders because it's exactly what they want. One of the main points of the initial Bitcoin whitepaper and further incarnations of other created coins and tokens is that their value is intrinsic to the currency itself and the people who hold it. It is not tied to the rise and fall of a certain country's economic standings or those of a bank. In many ways, crypto's popularity in the US can be traced directly back to the housing bubble collapse of the late 2000s that saw several enormous banks either collapse or need bailouts from the federal government. Getting the bailouts were all well and good for the fat cats living life in the C-suite of places like Wells Fargo, Bank of America, Morgan Stanley, Citigroup, and Goldman Sachs. But what about the people who saw their hard-earned 401(k) and other retirement savings literally collapse in a matter of days? According to a survey by Hewlett, more than half the people age 60 lost more than 20% of their 401(k) and IRA value during that time. That means if you were a year or two from retirement and had $500,000 waiting to be cashed out of your IRA, you might have watched $100,000 of it vanish in a week or two because a bunch of banks got so greedy that they stopped employing minimum standards in who was truly qualified to receive a loan to buy a home. Is there any wonder why so many people have gotten interested in cryptocurrency—which relies on neither banks nor government institutes?

Who's On First?

Although not exactly surprising, the first struggle that the US government has had with cryptocurrency is determining which government body in the US should even oversee its regulation. To date the US Department of the Treasury, the Securities and Exchange Commission (SEC), the Federal Trade Commission (FTC), the Internal Revenue Service (IRS), and the Financial Crimes Enforcement Network (FinCEN) all have different definitions of what cryptocurrency even means, as well as how it should be regulated.

FinCEN has stood by its assertion that cryptocurrency is not legal tender, but does consider crypto exchanges to be money transmitters, and thus subject to its jurisdiction. A bureau of the Department of the Treasury, FinCEN oversees battling money laundering, terrorist financing, and other financial crimes. Among US agencies, it is perhaps the most progressive and responsive to cryptocurrency, having added the phrasing "other value that substitutes for currency" to its usage of money services businesses as far back as July 2011. In March 2013, FinCEN unveiled its first guidance on virtual currencies, stating that 'exchangers and administrators' of virtual currency were legally considered money transmitters and would be compelled to comply with rules that prevented the financing of terrorists and money laundering. This language specifically did not require individuals from being charged with this same responsibility. That led to individuals using cryptocurrency, namely Bitcoin, for exactly that purpose to commit crimes and move illegal products. The aforementioned Silk Road and Ransomware crime reigns of the 2010s featured hundreds or thousands of individuals moving money through Bitcoin without having to reveal their real identities.

While FinCEN appeared initially on top of the situation, how to monitor, understand, and apprehend wrongdoers led to a myriad of task forces and groups all stepping on each other's feet as the US government tried to ascertain what threats there were from cryptocurrency. Among those that tried to sort out the heads and tails of the situation included the:

- Congress-run Bank Secrecy Act Advisory Group
- FBI-run Virtual Currency Emerging Threats Working Group
- FDIC-run Cyber Fraud Working Group
- Terrorist Financing & Financial Crimes-led Treasury Cyber Working Group

Keep in mind those four were all formed in about 18 months with different goals, different leadership, and different forms of accountability.

The financial government body that Americans are most familiar with—and usually react to about the same as someone scratching their nails on a chalkboard—is the IRS. The body that collects taxes from just about everything American citizens do was a bit slow on the uptake with crypto, not starting to turn over stones until 2013. At that point it suddenly went to court and filed a "John Doe" summons—meaning one that applied to anyone that fulfilled certain parameters, those being people who had used the trade exchange Coinbase to buy, sell, send or receive at least $20,000 worth of cryptocurrency in any one year between 2013 and 2015. This was a warning shot across the bow by the IRS letting individuals and corporations know that it is making a point to go after the biggest fish in the market—those investing —and presumably profiting—by buying and selling something the government deemed as a commodity without giving a percentage of that sale to the government in the form of taxes.

A year later, the IRS put out its first official statement, Notice 2014-21, also known as the Virtual Currency Guidance. A six-page document. In this notice, the IRS reiterated that virtual currency had no legal tender status in any jurisdiction in the US, but that Bitcoin was classified as a convertible virtual currency, meaning it had a basis in US dollars, euros, etc. Then, the little document dropped the bomb on crypto users, that virtual currency would be treated as if it were property and that general tax principles that applied to property transactions would also apply to virtual currency. Furthermore, anyone receiving virtual currency as payment for goods or services must include the fair market value of that currency in computing their gross yearly income. This fact included anyone who mined cryptocurrency. The property designation sent crypto traders largely for a loop. They argued it would hinder crypto from ever gaining widespread adoption because it was now being taxed in at least two ways, not to mention that it had been already defined by the Foreign Account Tax Compliance Act (FATCA) as existing inside cryptocurrency exchanges which were classified as financial institutions. This suggests the only things traded there are commodities or currencies, of which property is neither.

The IRS had the counter-argument—the only one that really matters given its de facto status as the tax authority in the US. The organization has five characteristics that must be met to define something as property. They are that it is:

- Definable
- Identifiable by third parties
- Capable of assumption by third parties
- Has a degree of permanence and persistence
- Grants the person holding it with the right for legal protection for third parties.

All of which are characteristics of cryptocurrency as defined by the initial whitepaper and arguments about the positives of crypto in the years leading up to the IRS's decision. The one positive of that decision is that cryptocurrency could be invested in a retirement account on a tax-deferred basis.

About eight months after the IRS Notice was released, the US Department of the Treasury announced it would solicit comments on how to properly report virtual currency as a Specified Foreign Financial Asset—despite the IRS saying something completely different in the same year!

The IRS continued to go after suspicious activity and in 2016, its investigation of Arthur Budovsky, founder of the digital currency service called Liberty Reserve, ended in him being sentenced to 20 years in federal prison for conspiracy to commit money laundering. The scheme had 78 million transactions with a combined value of $8 billion which were used to hide proceeds of Ponzi schemes, hacks, identity fraud, and credit-card theft.

Later that year, the IRS got an awakening of its own when the Treasury Inspector General for Tax Administration (TIGTA) warned the body that it needed better guidance on the tax implications of virtual currency transactions. It took another body blow the following summer when the IRS Taxpayer Advocate released a report calling the FAQs attached to the organization's original notice were a "trap for the unwary" because they were nonbinding.

In early 2018, Bitcoin's price busted the $10,000 ceiling and rose as high as $13,000. The IRS went on the offensive again, sending out a reminder to taxpayers that they were required to report virtual currency transactions on their income tax returns, and not doing so would be viewed as tax evasion, which carries with it a fine of up to $250,000 or three years in prison. Just four months later, as Americans began flocking to overseas cryptocurrency exchanges, the IRS doubled down on this assertion by altering the text of its Withholding and International Individual Compliance Area to read "US persons are subject to tax on worldwide income from all sources, including transactions involving virtual currency."

Meanwhile, the SEC had its own ideas about cryptocurrency, namely that it should be classified as a security, which would conveniently put the SEC in charge of its regulation. It went on to say that it was looking to make security laws apply to digital wallets and exchanges.

On the flip side of all this potential oversight is the stance taken by the Commodities Futures Trading Commission (CFTC). The CFTC is an independent agency that regulates futures, swaps, and different kinds of options. Its policy is to adopt a "do no harm" methodology saying that Bitcoin and other cryptocurrencies are commodities and that their derivatives can be traded publicly.

All of that appears about as clear as mud, which brings us to the last few years of decision making by the US government's various entities as pertains to cryptocurrency.

Modern IRS Updates

In October 2019, the IRS released its Revenue Ruling 2019-24 which updated multiple FAQs about virtual currency transactions and discussed the tax implications of air drops and hard forks. Hard forks have been previously defined and discussed in this text. An air drop is typically a marketing method used by a startup or a newcomer to the cryptocurrency market that sends tokens or coins to a digital wallet to introduce potential investors to that currency. This is typically done for free or in exchange for some sort of organic promotion such as sharing a link or a message about the cryptocurrency on social media. This was the first major release by the IRS in more than five years. For hard forks, the IRS addressed two situations. The first is when a hard fork occurs and the taxpayer receives no new cryptocurrency, and the second is when a hard fork is followed by an air drop of a new cryptocurrency and the taxpayer receives new crypto. It ruled that if crypto that is air dropped to an exchange that does not support, the individual does not have to count it as gross income and pay taxes on it. The same is true if a hard fork occurs that leaves you with the same amount of crypto, even if it's a different type.

However, the same document shutdown the idea of a minimum transaction amount to be taxable by the government when using crypto to purchase goods or services. Since the IRS is classifying cryptocurrency as property, it says that sales tax applies, using the theory that tax would be charged whether you were buying one square foot of a plot of land or 10,000 square feet.

In May 2020, the IRS put out a statement of work soliciting "consulting services to support a taxpayer examination involving virtual currency." In plain English, that means that the IRS is hiring outside contractors who know cryptocurrency to begin identifying crypto investors who are not reporting their transactions correctly or at all. That would suggest an increase in audits is headed your way, although that process might have been stagnated by COVID-19.

Blockchain Regulation

Although Bitcoin is the media darling, the blockchain technology itself has a much wider potential as has been mentioned in previous chapters—everything from IP management to financial services to medical records and energy use has already started to take shape in its innovation. Not surprisingly, there is no global regulation for blockchain in place, as different countries are simply making their own laws about its use in some cases, and leaving them up to individual states/regions or even companies themselves in others.

Chapter 10
Cryptocurrency and Taxes

In its first five years of existence, Bitcoin and the cryptocurrencies that followed it, offered a sanctuary free from tax concerns for investors. The long reach of the Internal Revenue Service did not invade the crypto space with either recognition or guidance on the subject. But far be it for the IRS to not want a piece of the action when someone inside US borders is making a profit. In 2014, the tax-collecting juggernaut finally weighed in on the subject, declaring that the tax classification of cryptocurrency going forward would be as a property, not a currency.

The ramifications of this decision, both for cryptocurrency holders and the IRS itself, are many, but things are far from cut and dried on either end. This chapter on cryptocurrency will:

- Investigate the current laws and how cryptocurrency owners are responding to them
- Present an overview of how individuals should pay taxes on cryptocurrency
- Suggest best practices to minimize cryptocurrency taxes owed

By classifying Bitcoin and other cryptocurrencies as property, the IRS demands that owners pay taxes each time they sell crypto. Depending on how involved you are in buying/selling crypto and with the price of those cryptocurrencies changing second to second all day long, keeping track of every single sale for every single person sounds implausible at best.

Things get even more tricky if you're using Bitcoin as an investment. If you hold it for less than a year before selling, the IRS will charge you income tax only. If you hold the cryptocurrency for more than a year and sell it, you'll have to pay capital gains taxes as high as 20% to the IRS.

The pressure to pay heavy tax rates has sent some crypto investors to use foreign exchanges or to move their funds to privacy coins—those that offer a higher degree of anonymity.

By handcuffing how citizens can use Bitcoin as a currency, the IRS began driving how they would view it, with more and more taking a long-term investment view over the alternate currency approach. In doing this, the IRS is also discouraging the incentive for cryptocurrencies to invest in infrastructure to make reporting to the IRS easier.

Just because it's the new kid on the block doesn't mean the IRS is using kid gloves when it comes to dealing with cryptocurrency. In 2017, the IRS began taking a closer look at the country's cryptocurrency exchanges seeking examples of tax fraud. That November, a federal judge in San Francisco ordered Coinbase to honor a summons to identify more than 14,000 accounts totaling nearly 9 million transactions between 2013-2015. The IRS was specifically targeting accounts that sent or received coins in excess of $20,000.

How to Pay Taxes on Cryptocurrency

The IRS refers to Bitcoin and the like as virtual currency transactions. These transactions are treated the same as transactions involving property. Taxpayers not reporting these transactions on their income tax can be liable for both interest and penalties.

Even though cryptocurrency is defined as property, the types of transactions it can be associated with cause it to immediately be split into different tax definitions. Here's a primer of what each kind of cryptocurrency event qualifies as according to the IRS.

- Trading cryptocurrencies: Produce capital gains or losses, must be reported as such on tax return.
- Paying with cryptocurrency: A tax event that can cause capital gains or capital losses. Is either short, or long-term capital gains based on the holding period.
- Receiving payment in crypto: In exchange for goods, services, or as a salary. This is considered ordinary income and does not need capital gains taxes.

If those were the only uses of cryptocurrency, the case would be cut and dry, but traders know better. Cryptocurrency extends far beyond into processes such as Bitcoin mining, air drops, ICOs and forked coins.

Bitcoin mining has been defined by the IRS as self-employment income, as the taxpayer is using his or her own hardware and processing power. It therefore is taxed as self-employment income.

Air drops and hard forks can befuddle even the most seasoned IRS employees, considering they are getting something for nothing; defined as new cryptocurrency distributed to existing owners. The IRS' stance is that this "new" currency must start with a price of $0, meaning whenever you sell it, you will pay a capital tax based on the final price.

Initial coin offerings (ICOs) are viewed as ordinary income and taxed as such.

The simplest way forward is to track all your cryptocurrency purchases and sales. This can be time consuming depending on how frequent a trader you are—cointracking.info is a great spreadsheet-enabled place to start—but can go a long way to combat IRS auditors. Accurate accounting must be applied to any tracking you do. A well-polished spreadsheet is like a security blanket; it's always there when you need it most.

Strategies to Minimize Crypto Taxes

Just like with any other income you make over the course of a tax year; you're going to look for ways to lessen your burden from the cryptocurrency profits you make. The first of these comes from any capital losses you've had on crypto, although you can't write off a loss of more than $3,000.

Another strategy on the ascend is to drive your IRA with Bitcoin and other cryptocurrencies. By opening a digital IRA and holding crypto inside of it, your taxes are delayed for as long as you hold the funds before taking a distribution.

The IRS might have been slow to get the ball rolling when it comes to classifying cryptocurrency inside of its tax environment, but the time has ended when investors can ignore how much they are spending and how much they are marking in cryptocurrency. The technology exists to make tracking your crypto a simpler process. Just as importantly, investors should keep on track of current tax policy, and any changes headed its way, as well as ways to minimize costs and connect deductions to your taxable income.

The IRS has never been the most predictable of organizations. Present figures suggest less than 1% of investors are reporting their crypto earnings to the IRS. The government isn't a fan of missing out on potential revenue, meaning it's only a matter of time before the IRS begins doling out punishments for underreporting and conducting audits of big traders to get its share.

Chapter 11
Cryptocurrency / NFTs in Sport

The news wires have been buzzing with the intermingling of cryptocurrency, blockchain and professional athletics in the past few years. Professional athletes are among the most well-paid individual workers in the world, and more and more of them are looking to invest and protect their money to avoid losing it in large amounts to taxes, while protecting it from the up-and-down volatility of the various stock markets that are so explicitly tied to socio-political comings and goings that have little to do with the actual markets.

In April 2021, cryptocurrency was splashed all over the front pages of websites and TV networks such as ESPN, Fox Sports, and Sports Illustrated, a decidedly uncharacteristic home for such financial pieces. The reason? It was the first night of the always anticipated NFL draft, and No. 1 overall pick Trevor Lawrence, after being selected by the Jacksonville Jaguars, announced he was going to partner with crypto investment app Blockfolio to invest his $22.63 million signing bonus in bitcoin, ether, and dogecoin. In a statement announcing the decision, Lawrence told media members. "When it comes to my crypto portfolio, I wanted a long-term partner in the space that I could trust." Lawrence also announced he is investing in the blockchain company Solana, which dubs itself as "a fast, secure, and censorship resistant blockchain providing the open infrastructure required for global adoption." For advocates of cryptocurrency as a viable, practical, and safe investment fund, Lawrence's announcement is a dream come true. Lawrence has been in the national spotlight since he came on the scene as a high school quarterback in Cartersville, Georgia. He led his high school to back-to-back state championships and was ranked as the No. 1 high school recruit in the country, standing 6-feet, 6-inches tall and sporting long hair that turned plenty of heads. He signed with national powerhouse Clemson and was the team's backup quarterback through the first four games of his freshman year. He took over for the incumbent starter and led the team to an undefeated record including a victory in the National Championship game over Alabama. Lawrence was named Offensive MVP of the game, the first freshman quarterback to win the national title game in 33 years. He led Clemson back to the National Championship game in 2019, ultimately winning 29 straight games before losing to LSU. In the shortened 2020 season, he was the Heisman Trophy runner-up and led the team to a 9-1 record, falling in the national semifinals. For his career, Lawrence went 34-2 with 90 touchdowns. This made him a shoo-in to be the #1 pick in the NFL draft and he has drawn comparisons to legendary quarterbacks like John Elway and Peyton Manning. As of April 2021, Lawrence has 931,000 Instagram followers. Making the giant splash into pro football and doing it alongside his big crypto investment has doubled up Lawrence's celebrity while putting extra emphasis on crypto, particularly ether and dogecoin, which has seen its market capitalization rise by more than 7,000% through the first four months of 2021 to some $50 billion, the fifth-highest among cryptocurrencies. It probably won't be "just" the $22 million signing bonus that Lawrence puts into cryptocurrency, either. He has also inked deals with Bose, Gatorade, Adidas, and sports memorabilia company Fanatics. Lawrence is an advertiser's dream—tall, good looking, intelligent, well-spoken, and proud of his Christian faith. He's already a family man as well, despite being only 22 years old. He married his high school sweetheart three weeks before being drafted. All those characteristics make him a great figure for crypto fans to rally around. A top-flight football player like Lawrence obviously has legal and financial advisors on his team. Making the initial high-profile investment into cryptocurrency and blockchain is a breath of fresh air for the industry.

Lawrence isn't the first National League Football Player to get interested, either. In 2020, defensive lineman Russell Okung of the Carolina Panthers announced he was using half of his NFL salary to buy bitcoin. Okung, a native of Houston, TX, played college football at Oklahoma State University. He was drafted in the first round of the 2013 NFL Draft and helped the Seattle Seahawks win their first Super Bowl title as a rookie. He also founded the Greater Organization in 2016, which has the mission of using technology to provide access and opportunity for underserved youth. In the year since, he has expressed more and more interest in entrepreneurship and cryptocurrency, going as far as to request being paid his salary in 2019 in bitcoin. He was denied this request, but the same year started his own Bitcoin brand and events series called "Bitcoin is". His education of others about wanting to be paid in bitcoin resulted in his partnership with Strike to allow Okung to be the first pro athlete receiving bitcoin in exchange for his play on the field.

"Media is more than currency, it's power," Okung said when the announcement was revealed. The way money is handled from creation to dissemination is part of that power. Getting paid in bitcoin is the first step of opting out of the corrupt, manipulated economy we all inhabit. Bitcoiners are not only disrupting the status quo, we are reclaiming power that is rightly ours. This is the acknowledgement of a new way, a new path, and a new future that recognizes diversity in finance and a reclamation of true financial control."

Following in Okung's footsteps, Kansas City Chiefs' tight end Sean Culkin plans to convert his entire 2021 salary of $920,000 into bitcoin. Culkin revealed in an interview that he was influenced by his father's own investment habits growing up and got even more interested in finance while in college at the University of Missouri.

"I've always had a lot of interest in and a passion for finances and economics from my days at Mizzou," Culkin told ESPN in April 2021. "Even before that, my dad was big, really bullish on gold. Early on, I was always exposed to his philosophies on what made gold an intractable investment looking at it from a macro perspective. There's a lot of overlap between gold and Bitcoin. I really spent all my time in the offseason the past year just hearing about this growing space in crypto. It just seemed like it was getting bigger and bigger." Culkin turned heads on social media earlier in 2021 when he speculated that if he had turned his 2017 rookie signing bonus of $12,000 into bitcoin, it would be worth $250,000 today.

It's not just players getting invested in cryptocurrency, however. In early April 2021, the Sacramento Kings announced they would be offering bitcoin to all players and coaches for the 2021-2022 season as a direct form of payment should they so desire. The idea is the brainchild of Kings' co-owner and chairman Vivek Yashwant Ranadive, an Indian-American business executive who is also the founder of TIBCO Software and Teknekron Software Systems. Innovation has long been a staple of Ranadive's story. In the 1970s he was accepted to MIT while living in India, but the Indian government refused to release foreign currency for him to study abroad. He was able to talk his way into the office of the Reserve Bank of India and get the funds released. He is a huge advocate of real-time technology, which explains part of his fascination with cryptocurrency and blockchain. He purchased the team in 2013, and the following year, the Kings became the first professional sports team to accept bitcoin for tickets or merchandise payments. The Dallas Mavericks, owned by renegade billionaire Mark Cuban, followed suit in 2019, and in 2021, Cuban announced that dogecoin is now also acceptable by the Mavericks. Cuban, who has owned the Mavericks since 2000, is a leading voice in the American investment space and worth more than $4.3 billion.

If Lawrence is the hunky future of cryptocurrency, Cuban is the rebellious face of the present. He has long defied the odds and the standards of being a leading financial wizard in the US, starting with his massive deal that made his net worth reach 10 figures way back in 2000 when he sold Broadcost.com to Yahoo for $5.7 billion of the company's stock. Showing an extremely shrewd intellect, Cuban turned around and hedged against the stock's future decline, getting really rich just before the dot.com bubble burst.

As well known as he already was after buying the Mavericks and repeatedly defying the league's commissioners with his unorthodox comments and practices, his spotlight grew infinitely larger when he joined the cast of the American TV series "Shark Tank". A spinoff of the UK's "Dragon's Den", the show features Cuban as one of five billionaire investors who get pitched investment ideas by up-and-coming entrepreneurs. Upon hearing the contestants' elevator pitches and asking a few questions, Cuban and his fellow "Sharks" make offers on investing in the company—or turn them down. Cuban joined the show in its second season and has been on it ever since, including for all three years that it has won an Emmy Award. His combination of brutal honesty and sympathy makes him among the show's most popular hosts.

While JPMorgan was making its famous condemnation of cryptocurrency and Bitcoin, only to turn that around recently, Cuban has been more open-minded and positive about the cryptocurrency industry from the get-go. In 2021, he has become a leading voice of the industry potential as a smart investment. In an April 2021 interview, with UpOnly, Cuban went on record as saying Bitcoin would start gobbling up some of gold's map market.

"Bitcoin's great as a platform. It's accepted now. It's an alternative asset. It's going to replace gold in the portfolios of a lot of people and that hopefully will push the price up as long as the whales continue to HODL. But that's a different type of platform and its utility really only happens when you wrap it, at least as of now," Cuban said.

"You're starting to see these [exchange-traded funds] pop up and ways for people to buy it. It's too difficult still to get money into a wallet just to buy Bitcoin. So you need to have somebody that you can work with that is going to hold it for you, right? Because most people are going to be terrified of having that Bitcoin in their own custody. And so until that's simple, people are going to want to buy it through traditional means – through their broker, or through Robinhood even, Coinbase to a lesser extent, but just that process of going through the Know-Your-Customer (KYC, AML stuff and connecting to your bank – it's still too much of a hassle right now. It's just easier for people to deal with a stock brokerage. But as there is more and more opportunity for people to buy from people they already have their savings with and their retirements with, you're going to see it chip away at gold. Because the reality is gold is sold off of narrative just like Bitcoin is. And it's really built on trust – do you trust gold or do you trust Bitcoin? Younger generations are going to trust Bitcoin because gold has no utility in and of itself. What is gold good for? It's good for nothing."

Although he is bullish on Bitcoin, Cuban is known in cryptocurrency circles as being someone who firmly believes there is room for more than one seat at the table of future success in the industry. Appealing on the Unchained podcast in early April 2021, Cuban said that he was onboard with what have otherwise been hailed as controversial upgrades to Ethereum's network, saying he believes they will make the blockchain platform more eco-friendly and that it will eventually allow Ethereum to "dwarf" blockchain in terms of applications. Ethereum announced earlier this year it was making major changes to its network that would not only limit transaction fees for users but also start to burn coins, upsetting many of its miners. Its developers are interested in moving the system of verifying transactions to a proof of stake model. Cuban believes the Ethereum blockchain's multiple uses—including smart contracts and non-fungible tokens (NFTs) are going to allow it to create more financial contracts without needing third-party intervention, thus gaining more acceptances into day-to-day society.

"I think the applications leveraging smart contracts and extensions on Ethereum will dwarf bitcoin," Cuban was quoted as saying. "That doesn't mean I'm going to sell my Bitcoin. I'm not. But at the same time, let's just say I own a lot more Ether than I do bitcoins. In a few years, I think Ethereum and maybe 2 or 3 other blockchains will have their place, and those will be the winners."

It's a far cry from Cuban's early days in cryptocurrency when he called it too complicated and famously quoted he would "rather have bananas than bitcoin." He's come around in the last few years, praising the decentralized finance (DeFi) marketplace. He has told his own investors that if he had it all to do over again, he would build his businesses around blockchain technology, smart contracts, and NFTs. He's hardly all talk, either. In the first quarter of 2021, Cuban invested in the NFT platforms SuperRare, Mintable, CryptoSlam, and OpenSea. Cuban walks the walk, using a Coinbase wallet to buy coins for his portfolio. He bought shares of Coinbase the day it debuted on NASDAQ. CryptoSlam seems like the perfect venue for the owner of the Dallas Mavericks, who are enjoying a resurgence in 2021 behind the outstanding play of rising superstar Luka Doncic.

CryptoSlam is an aggregator of NFT collectible data from the likes of the Ethereum, WAX, and FLOW blockchains. Founded by CEO Randy Wasinger, CryptoSlam started up in 2018. Its first venue was with MLB Champions, the first NFTs to be officially licensed by a major professional sports league. CryptoSlam is currently tracking more than 50 NFT projects from a trio of blockchains. Its biggest start of 2021 has been NBA Top Shot.

What are NFTs?

You're not alone if you've struggled to dissect what NFTs are and how they work. For starters, the acronym contains a phrase "non-fungible" that isn't exactly household investing 101.

Fungible on its own is a term to describe a quality of a commodity that can have a part, a whole, or a quantity, replaced by an equal number of parts when paying a debt or settling an account. If John lends Bill $20 for lunch, Bill can replay John with a different $20 tomorrow and it's worth the exact same amount. The same thing goes for more natural commodities. If a furniture store in Texas purchases three tons of wood from a lumber mill in Colorado, but the mill only has 2.5 tons on hand, it can buy the other one-half ton from another mill in Wyoming and fill the order to complete satisfaction.

With that definition in mind, the opposite, non-fungible, is more readily understandable. Non-fungible then means that a commodity cannot be replaced by any other commodity. If you have a painting by Pablo Picasso in your boardroom and it gets stolen, your property management company cannot replace it with something they found at a flea market last Saturday. In fact, they cannot even replace it with another Picasso or similar rare work of art because the properties of the singular painting do not exist anywhere else in the world. There are many things that share similarities with it, but nothing else is the exact same work.

By extension, non-fungible tokens (referred to as NFTs for the duration of this book), are cryptographic assets that exist in a blockchain that have one-of-a-kind metadata and identification codes to tell them apart from everything else. As such, they are unique in the blockchain environment because they cannot be traded or exchanged at any sort of equivalency rate, unlike cryptocurrency, which exists in precisely that fashion. NFTs can be used to represent real-world items such as any sort of collectible, artwork, or property. When an item is tokenized—it means that an NFT is created to represent it in the blockchain environment. Ownership of the token represents ownership of the actual item as well. Once it takes on a form in the blockchain, it can be more easily sold, bought, or traded efficiently using smart contracts and the associated security that comes on the blockchain, which can greatly reduce the risk of fraud for these high-dollar items. NFTs are not only for collectibles or real estate, however. They can also contain people's personal identities, property rights, and other legal qualifications that otherwise require a third party to transfer.

NFTs different from normal tokens in the amount of information they store. Anything that can be stored digitally, including digital art, photographs, music files, videos, video game characters, etc., qualifies. For the time being, NFTs exist solely on Ethereum's blockchain. That's doing wonders for Ethereum's market value. In early May 2021, the cryptocurrency jumped above a record high of $3,500 and analysts were targeting a new plateau of $5,200 before encountering serious resistance. Through the first four months of 2021, ether rose 363% compared to bitcoin's 87% rise through the same first quarter. While Bitcoin was still valued more than 12 times as much as Ethereum in early May 2021, there is starting to be more and more of a deviation of what each cryptocurrency company represents—Bitcoin holds value like gold or some other rare commodity, while Ethereum is finding more and more ways to integrate itself into people's everyday financial transactions.

As for NFTs, they soared into the public vernacular in March 2021 when Mike Winkelmann, an artist more well-known as Beeple, sold a digital painting called "Everydays: The First 5000 Days" for $69.3 million, the third-highest price ever for a living artist. The transaction was done using an NFT through Christie's Auction House. Prior to last October, Winklemann had never sold a print for more than $100, but in October he sold his first series of NFTs for $66,666.66 each. In December, he sold another series of work for $3.5 million. It's not just Winklemann, either. One of his first NFTs from October 2020 resold in March 2021 for $6.6 million. There are plenty of different theories on why the prices have spiked so high for an artist who was making a nice living, but certainly not anything so extravagant until a few months ago. Owning the rights to a work of art gives a buyer "bragging rights" for being the only one who can legally display it as well as acquiring an asset they can sell later. In the case of digital art, there's no concern of the value degrading due to wear and tear, either. Beeple has mastered the art of catering to the 21st century artist. He has more than 2.5 million followers across his social channels, and Everydays is a famous project that is a conglomeration of his ongoing project in which he creates and publishes a new piece of digital artwork every single day. As of the time of this writing in May 2021, Beeple has created digital artwork for 5,117 consecutive days —more than 14 years straight.

The fervent rush to collect and sell digital artwork in NFT form is not without its problems. Lots of artwork of questionable value is being auctioned off in an attempt to drive high prices. Lots of artists are having their work stolen and auctioned off by unlicensed third parties. So where can you buy NFTs for merchandise and collectibles? Currently there are nine sites offering them. They include:

OpeanSea: OpenSea bills itself as the world's largest NFT marketplace, with collections of digital art, virtual worlds, collectibles, and the ability for anyone to either set up a wallet, create a collection, add your own NFTs, or list them for sale as auctions, fixed-price listings, or declining-price listings. There are also categories for domain names, trading cards, and sports collectibles. OpenSea got its start in 2017.

SuperRare: SuperRare Digital Artworks operates by having artists authenticate their artwork by digitally signing it when creating a tokenized certificate. They then set a price or let collectors bid on their art in a marketplace. As of May 2021, it is in early-access phase where it is only allowing hand-picked artists to sell on its platform, but is planning a full launch in 2022. SuperRare sold the first digital home for $500,000. Designed by Krista Kim, a Toronto-based artist, it is hailed as the first digital house in the world, created by an architect and a video-game software company. Using virtual reality, the buyer can explore the mansion, which is "located" on Mars, and sunbathe outside the house in Mars' atmosphere.

Nifty Gateway: Nifty Gateway hails itself as the premier marketplace for "Nifties," which it defines as digital items that can have real ownership. Nifties live on a blockchain so that they can never completely vanish, although the things that make them unique still could. For instance, if you store access to a World of Warcraft character as an NFT, but World of Warcraft stops being a game to be played, the NFT would be essentially worthless without the platform to utilize it.

Foundation: Named for the visionary Isaac Asimov series of books by the same title, Foundation is a stylized auction house that has current bids in ether and countdown clocks on every item it stores. It hails itself as the new creative economy, bringing 'digital creators, crypto natives, and collectors together to move culture forward.' Foundation advertises its digital creators as much as it does their creations, giving them brightly colored profiles on the front page with the ability to be followed much like on social media. Foundation thinks of itself as a Decentralized Autonomous Organization (DAO), a group of people who share a common goal and use blockchain to make decisions. DAOs have the unique advantage over a typical business operation of being autonomous without human interaction with rules that exist before deployment, much the same way a software system works. When certain criteria are met, the DAO acts accordingly. DAO strengths include anonymity, autonomy, efficiency, and transparency.

VIV3: With a very similar setup to Foundation, VIV3 allows artists, brands, and game studios to mint tokens for their digital creations. It is Flow's first digital marketplace. Founded by Daniel Podaru and Ilya Siban, it was launched in January 2021 and allows users to buy/sell, trade, and track the digital history of NFTs.

BakerySwap: BakerySwap uses a unique, old-fashioned home page set up to sell art cards, digital art, gaming resources, and more. It heavily features top users to give more of a community feel.

Some brands have jumped onboard right away with NFTs, including the fast-food restaurant Taco Bell, which produced a series of taco-themed GIFs and images. These NFTs included $500 gift cards to Taco Bell, and the series sold out in 30 minutes, with some going on secondary markets for as high as $3,500. In late April 2021, the Golden State Warriors announced a legacy NFT collection series called the Warriors Championship Ring NFTs and the Commemorative Ticket Stub NFTs. The NFTs will be combined with physical items, which include a custom championship ring presentation and an experience called "Warrior-for-a-Day". The ring NFT features the team's six NBA Championship Rings reproduced as limited edition NFTs. The bidder who purchases the first edition of each ring will receive a corresponding physical Warriors Championship Ring from the team's 1947,

1956, 1975, 2015, 2017 or 2018 NBA Championships. An additional token, the 1-of-1 Warriors Six-Time NBA Champion Ring, will allow the winning bidder to receive a one-of-a-kind physical ring created by jeweler Jason of Beverly Hills. The team's ticket collection will feature digital representations of ticket stubs from some of the franchise's greatest games including several at the tail end of championships won.

What are the advantages of moving NFTs as compared to other assets? Here are several reasons why many investors and collectors are keen on the idea of utilizing them.

1. Standardization: Traditional digital assets have no real representation in the real world. You see them bartered on message boards, social media platforms, eBay, etc. Converting them to NFTs on blockchain gives them certain inalienable rights like ownership, access control, and the power to transfer them that has not previously existed.

2. Interoperability: NFT standards allow for the tokens to move across multiple ecosystems with relative ease. They are viewable inside multiple wallet providers, marketplaces, and inside virtual worlds, a relatively new development. Because the API for reading and writing data on blockchain is already fairly-well defined, the open standards provide for an API that is consistent, reliable, and clear when it comes to reading and writing data.

3. Tradability: Free trade on open marketplaces without the need for a third party is perhaps the most exciting features of NFTs. Game developers can transition from a closed economy to an open, free-market one. They can be bought, sold and traded in eBay style auctions, through the use of stablecoins, in currencies specific to a certain application, or through any other style of financial transaction.

4. Liquidity: With the ability to be instantly traded, NFTs become liquid assets that can be sold at a moment's notice if need be. This is the birth of a new asset class that expands the market for unique digital assets like few before it.

5. Provable Scarcity: Smart contracts let developers put hard caps on

the supply of NFTs so that only a specific number of a rare item is created, which keeps supply in check.

6. Programmability: Most of today's NFT's have mechanics built in for forging, crafting, redeeming, or random generation.

A Brief History of NFTs

The first experimental NFTs were a group of colored coins called Rare Pepes, using an illustration of Pepe the Frog that were sold on eBay and later at a live auction. The first Ethereum-based NFT experiment was called CryptoPunks, 10,000 unique collectible punks with their own set of unique characteristics. Built by Larva Labs, CryptoPunks inhabited an on-chain marketplace and are today thought of as digital antiques. The unlikely true starting point of NFTs in the mainstream was the birth of CryptoKitties, a late 2017 creation at the ETH Waterloo hackathon. It was an on-chain game that allowed users to 'breed' digital cats together to make new cats of different degrees of rarity. The first cats—"Generation 0" were auctioned off in a Netherlands-based declining auction, with new cats sold on a secondary market. Many in the gaming community called CrypoKitties not a real game, but its supporters disagreed, in large part because of its speculative mechanics and viral story. The mechanics of the game were clear cut and showed an easy way to make a profit. Buy two cats, breed them to make a rarer cat, sell the new cat, and repeat the process. The second and future generation of cats often were sold on secondary markets, which was likely the genesis for many of the NFT platforms we see today. The most expensive legitimate sale was 253 ETH (about $110,000) of Founder Cat #18. The niche of CryptoKitties came from them being fun, cute, and shareable. Regardless of what people's interests are in finance, crypto, or programming, there are certain things that everyone can agree on; and a fun game that's a little bit competitive and a little bit quirky scratched the right itch at the right time. Of course, the bubble soon popped although the market still does some business each week.

A number of imitators called "layer two" games followed CryptoKitties using the same experience but without any ties to the original software. They included Kitty Race, where you could race your CryptoKitties against each other, and KittyHats, which allowed you to accessorize your CryptoKitties. This was followed up by a hot-potato game called CryptoCelebrities in which a collectible celebrity NFT was created. Once it was sold to someone else for a higher price, the seller earned the difference. Each time someone was willing to buy the celebrity NFT, the previous person made money, but once the price got too high, the last person was the one holding the hot potato and effectively "got burned."

In early 2018, venture capitalists and crypto funds got interested in NFTs and blockchain game studio Lucid Sight raised $6 million while Forte and Ripple combined to $100 million for a blockchain gaming fund. Nonfungible.com started an NFT tracking platform in 2018, but things still didn't really take off until later that year when digital art platforms began emerging, and artists like JOY and Josie started their own contracts to brand themselves in the new industry. In the summer of 2018, Digital Art Chain became the first platform that allowed users to mint NFTs out of their digital images. By 2019, the Kred platform was letting influences create coupons, collectibles, and coupons.

As briefly mentioned previously, Major League Baseball was the first sporting association to get into NFTs, joining in a partnership with Lucid Sight in April 2018 for an on-chain baseball game called MLB Crypto. Since then, Formula 1 race cars have launched F1 Delta Time, Paramount has fired up the Star Trek game CryptoSpaceCommanders, and there are multiple sports trading card companies in the realm including Sorare and Stryking. Internationally, Japanese games have taken the plunge with an RPG game called MyCryptoHeroes that has a complex in-game economy. Users can transfer their characters to Ethereum to sell them if they so choose. The virtual world Cryptovoxels involves simple web-based virtual reality to show off a gallery of your digital art.

Trading card games have also joined the ranks of NFTs. Long-time games like Magic the Gathering have their own economies with lots of marketplaces and companion sites. A game like Hearthstone, which is the digital equivalent of Magic the Gathering, has started to use the NFT market to make its transactions easier and quicker.

NFT Criticism and Controversy

One of the early negatives that has found its way into the public forum is how much energy NFTs use in their creation. According to the website CryptoArt.wtf, which measures the carbon footprint of NFTs, an artwork called "Coronavirus" gobbled up 192 kWh of electricity during its creation process, which is about how much a person in the EU uses in two weeks. It's a problem that blockchain has overall. Ethereum's energy consumption has skyrocketed in the last half a year. On May 3, 2020, it was a bit under 8 TWh per year. On the same date in 2021, it had risen above 41 TWh per year. At that rate, Ethereum is consuming as much energy in a year as the entire country of New Zealand and leaving behind a carbon footprint the equivalent of Bolivia. A single Ethereum transaction uses as much energy as the average American home for 2.6 days and has the carbon footprint of 6,102 hours of watching YouTube.

Another criticism of NFTs as pertains to artists is that the modern platforms are using the same shortcut that the original inventors did, which is selling a link to the digital artwork original, not buying the actual original. What happens when the website that link lives on ends up failing? Moreover, many are confused by what is actually being purchased when you compare a digital original to a digital copy. With an original piece of art, there's a clear-cut definition between the original oil painting and a print of it made by a machine. For a lot of critics, buying an NFT feels suspiciously like owning bragging rights and not a lot more. That criticism came into play when Twitter's CEO Jack Dorsey sold his first tweet as an NFT for $2.9 million in 2021. How can someone possess a tweet? Other than hoping someone else wants to buy it for more money, where is its value? The winner of the auction for the tweet came from Sina Estavi, CEO of Bridge Oracle.

NBA Top Shot has proven to be a great synergy of sport and NFTs in 2021. The blockchain-based platform allows users to buy and sell officially licensed NBA collectible highlights called "Moments" which are highlight packages of players that are created and sold. In the first eight months of its existence, a highlight of LeBron James, the NBA's most famous active player and one of its all-time greats, sold for $200,000. Another of Zion Williamson, the #1 draft pick in the league in 2020, sold for just a bit less. The makers of this new venture? Dapper Labs—the same Canadian company that first brought CryptoKitties to life. Top Shot is billed as a crypto-collectible that consumers can purchase in the form of an NFT. Since no two Moments are the same, each one is a non-hackable, unique item. Even if someone makes a perfect copy of the highlight video, without having the token, it will instantly be known as being fake. The packs, as they are referred to, cost as few as $9 to buy when they are released, although they tend to sell out quickly. The company reported sales of $230 million in its first eight months, although most of that has come from traders exchanging the collectibles after they initially sold. Dapper's profits come from the initial sales of the NFTs and from a transaction fee that comes in the peer-to-peer dealings. The NBA also gets a cut of every deal, since it is the one originally providing the licensed footage. The deal between the pro league and Dapper Labs started in 2019. Dapper Labs digitizes the NBA's footage, which makes each package one of kind, and thus scarce. Some NFTs include different angles and interesting digital artwork, pushing up their value. There are lots of different strategies involved for traders seeking which players to go after. The current crop of superstars such as James and Williamson, Steph Curry, James Harden, and Kevin Durant, are all going for high prices from the get-go. These players are all perennial All-Stars with huge fan followings. The more interesting approach is to go after young players who have great potential, but haven't shown it on the court just yet. A big game or a big week can suddenly send a player's Highlight value shooting sky-high, at least for a few days. A good example of this is Kevin Porter Jr., a second-year player for the Houston Rockets. He was a first-round draft choice from USC and has had a decent season in 2021, but also ran afoul of league rules for violating COVID-19 safety policies and fined $50,000. However, just a week later, Porter became the fourth-youngest player to score 50 points in a game. In a few hours' time, his Moments went from selling for $6 to $6,000.

Mavericks' owner Mark Cuban is a big supporter of Top Shot, comparing it to the model of sports trading cards where consumers collected their favorite players year by year and also searched and traded for rare cards. Critics of Top Shot might wonder why fans are willing to pay for highlights of players they could see on YouTube or ESPN as many times as they want, but Cuban has the right of it. The tradability, the scarcity, and the collection aspects are all what is driving the business forward.

In its current incarnation, Top Shot is recreating the baseball card craze of the 1980s and 1990s to a tee. Baseball cards first appeared as early as the 1860s in the form of advertisements on products as baseball became America's first popular, national sport. A sporting goods company called Beck & Snyder in New York City sold the first set of baseball cards in 1868. As baseball and photography both gained popularity into the 20th century, most teams began releasing sets each year, eventually being usurped by companies like Bowman and Topps, which began in 1952, and a few years later, bought out Bowman. Topps had the equivalent of a national monopoly for decades after that, although smaller companies like Donruss and Fleer made regional sets to appeal to some fan bases. In 1980, those two companies sued and won freedom to print their own sets, with a court deeming Topps an unfair monopoly. This coincided at a unique time in American history. Baseball fans who had grown up watching the sport in the 1950s and 1960s were now entering their 40s and 50s. With disposable income to spare, they began seeking out and buying baseball cards from years gone by of their boyhood heroes like Mickey Mantle, Sandy Koufax, Willie Mays, and Hank Aaron. The cards were no different than they had been when they were originally sold for 5-15 cents 20-30 years earlier, but they were in short supply, particularly as the quality of the card went up. For all the colors and facts on the cards, they were still only made from a kind of hardened paper, and thus highly susceptible to wear and tear of age, the way they were stored, and any sort of spillage or exposure. By 1984, there were two separate magazines dedicated to pricing sports collectibles, with an extreme focus on baseball cards. As the industry saw more and more business, two more players—Score and Upper Deck—joined the fray, with Upper Deck understanding more than any other company seemingly how valuable mint condition cards were, and using tamper-proof packaging and holograms on the card to verify their authenticity. A first-year card issued by Upper Deck featured Seattle Mariners rookie Ken Griffey Jr., who not only made it to the major leagues at age 19, but also played alongside his own father, Ken Griffey, when the latter was 40 and 41 years old. The two made baseball history in 1990 when they hit back-to-back home runs in a game. Griffey's Upper Deck card has been sold at auction for more than $50,000.

The real impetus of the baseball card craze involved searching for rare cards featuring New York Yankee legend Mickey Mantle. His 1952 Topps card is considered the rarest of the post-World War II era, and one sold at auction in January 2021 for $5.2 million. Like Griffey nearly 40 years later, Mantle came up at a young age—making the Yankees roster in 1951 as a teenager and played at the epicenter of the sporting world for the next 18 years, winning the World Series seven times and being named Most Valuable Player of the league three times. At the time that Mantle was rising to superstardom, baseball was relegated to a Game of the Week shown on TV on Saturday afternoons. The only other time Americans could watch baseball on TV was during the World Series, where Mantle played 12 times in his career. Not surprisingly, Mantle became a legend to a generation of young men who wanted to recapture their youth through collecting baseball cards a generation later. Top Shot is the next incarnation of the cards' craze, just with more permanence because the Moments can't lose their quality by wear and tear.

Another move towards general cryptocurrency acceptance in 2021 came when the state of Wyoming legalized online sports betting with a law that will allow gamblers to place their wages in crypto. House Bill 133, signed into law by the state governor, decrees that sportsbooks may accept "digital, crypto, and virtual currencies" as long as those items can be converted into cash. Wyoming is the least populated state in the country, with just 578,759 residents as of 2019. That's fewer people than live in 31 American cities. But that's a good thing for crypto proponents. Having a state where gambling reigns supreme, like Nevada, New Jersey, or Louisiana being the first convert to crypto in a gambling context would invite much scrutiny and criticism, and any missteps would get blown out of proportion by the media. By having a much smaller cross-section be the initial adopters, it should be easier to iron out the kinks before moving to a larger-scale model in a city with more casinos and more gamblers. Wyoming's move is the next step of the state's push towards embracing digital currency. Previous legislation passed to woo crypto businesses and including crypto as a payment for local businesses just made sense from there.

"I think that Wyoming legislators are getting more comfortable with cryptocurrency as the issue evolves in our state," said state Sen. Jeff Wasserburger (R-Gillette), one of the bill's sponsors, in a state news conference.

In 2018, Wyoming's state legislature created and appointed the Wyoming Blockchain Task Force for the purpose of drafting proposed legislation for the state. The task force went to work in the 2018/2019 legislative session, during which time the state passed 13 crypto-friendly laws with the intention of making Wyoming the ideal destination for crypto companies and crypto/blockchain entrepreneurs. That movement gives Wyoming a distinct advantage over the other 49 states in the Union, making it the only one with a comprehensive legal framework that gives blockchain and cryptocurrency companies the structure, tax status, and infrastructure needed to hit the ground running. Innovation from individuals or companies is the new mantra of the day in Wyoming, which has brought an influx of investment, revenue, and new jobs to the state. Wyoming has identified itself as the "Delaware of digital asset law", a play on the idea that Delaware is the nation's leader in corporate law. Since Wyoming's passage of the 13 laws, more than a dozen other US states have passed at least 1 or 2 of the same bills for their states in an effort to also appeal to blockchain and cryptocurrency startups. But they're all behind the curve set by Wyoming, which has claimed the first-mover advantage and made the biggest splash.

Some of the key moves made by Wyoming's torrent of blockchain laws include:

1. The recognition of direct property rights for individual owners of any type of digital asset including currencies, securities, and utility tokens. Also applies the super-negotiable rules of commercial law to apply to virtual currencies, which in turn increase their liquidity, by applying the same rules to cryptocurrency that apply to money. Wyoming's commercial law was also adjusted to clearly define what digital assets are in terms of how they are owned and what characteristics they have; in this case, directly owned peer-to-peer assets.

2. The creation of a 'sandbox environment' for financial technology (fintech) companies to exist with regulatory relief from existing

laws for a period of up to three years.

3. The creation of a new state-chartered depository institution that gives basic banking services to blockchain and other cryptocurrency businesses. The bank must have 100% reserves and cannot lend money. It is expressly for business depositors and does not have to have FDIC insurance, although it is encouraged. The banks began opening in March 2020.

4. Allowed for Wyoming banks to become "qualified custodians" for digital assets from September 2019. Qualified custodian status meant that these banks recognize that they cannot treat digital assets like traditional securities.

Individuals with digital assets can get protected by Wyoming's new laws by moving to Wyoming, moving your cold storage to Wyoming, or set up an LLC, corporation, trust or foundation in Wyoming. Interestingly, Wyoming is also the state that invented the LLC in the first place. Its LLC laws have potent privacy protections, and Wyoming is often called the most tax-friendly state in the US.

There are three straightforward ways that businesses can benefit from Wyoming's generous blockchain laws. The first is to apply Wyoming law to your contracts involving digital assets, the second is to legally domicile in Wyoming, and the third is to physically locate your business in Wyoming. Another big advantage is that the state does not have a state income tax to drain company's revenue. The state frequently comes up as the No. 1 destination for tax purposes, as it also has no corporate income tax, franchise tax, or gross-receipt tax. There are currently 25 opportunity zones spread throughout Wyoming that allow you to use capital gains tax deferrals. One such company taking advantage of the tax breaks is Zytara, which announced it was entering the NFT market in April 2021. Based in Cheyenne, Wyoming, this fintech company plans to provide Generation Z and Millennial esports fans and gaming enthusiasts with the financial services to meet their needs for digital currency and financial institutions.

"The leading digital financial institutions of tomorrow will not only hold cash and traditional investments, they'll custody digital assets, including cryptocurrencies and NFTs," said Al Burgio, founder & CEO of Zytara in a press release. "Our latest expansion enables Zytara to also support strategic partners including esports teams, gamers, musical artists, actors, and other brands with the creation, sales and marketing of NFTs."

Zytara launched the Zytara dollar (ZUSD) as part of a partnership with Prime Trust. The ZUSD is a programmable money for the gaming industry with a 1:1 basis with US dollars.

Sports teams aren't just allowing payment in cryptocurrency, they're also starting to be tokenized. Chiliz is a blockchain company that has begun issuing tokens associated with sports teams. Based in Malta, Chiliz powers the Socios.com platform which offers tokens to soccer fans who then participate in polls hosted by their favorite clubs. Doing well in the polls allows the fans to receive either rewards or special promotions. The tokens are typically listed on Binance or on Korean exchanges.

"The Chiliz blockchain and our consumer-facing product Socios.com grew massively in the last few months in terms of users, user spending, but also in terms of new sports partners like AC Milan, FC Barcelona, and Manchester City," says Chiliz CEO Alexandre Dreyfus.

Chiliz has risen more than 2,100% in the first quarter of 2021, with a recent investing influence from Jump Trading, based out of Chicago.

Chapter 12
20 Biggest Names in Crypto/Blockchain Today

We've covered a lot of ground and covered a lot of important events that help define the history of blockchain and cryptocurrency to date. Here are some of the top names and faces that will define the industry over the next decade or more.

1. **Andre Cronje:** Despite most of his competition hitting the industry at an early age, Cronje is the official late bloomer of the bunch. He was a computer scientist at heart in the early 2000s while working as a lawyer. In the next decade, he started taking more and more classes and left law altogether in 2016 as he became fascinated by blockchain, eventually becoming a code reviewer and partner for Crypto Briefing before moving on to a technical adviser role with the Fantom Foundation. In 2020, he became a shiny new figure in crypto as he moved to working for Yearn Finance, single-handedly developing the yield aggregating platform on Ethereum. Its YFI token surged more than 300% in a single week in August of 2020 as the project started developing into an ecosystem of different protocols including Curve, Compound, dYdX, and Aave. In a single sentence, it diverts liquidity to different sectors of the DeFi in a mission to find the best returns on investment. It's not surprising that this is Cronje's baby considering he has been obsessed with DeFi and stablecoins for the past five years. His meticulous fascination with computer science saw him dissecting the code of other platforms to build his own. The first version of Yearn was Cronje managing money for friends and family. Cronje is passionate about his projects to the point that when he tires of them, he tends to light out of them in a hurry, just ask his previous law firm. For the meantime, he is one of the most dedicated prospectors in the industry, and anything he does should be watched closely.

2. **Sam Bankman-Fried:** This 29-year-old from Stanford, California is an MIT graduate and the founder and CEO of Alameda Research and FTX. Working out of Hong Kong, he sometimes

sleeps on a bean bag at work so he can recharge his body quickly and get back to doing what he does best, which is the cryptocurrency and derivatives exchange known as FTX. He has a degree in physics from MIT, graduating in 2014. After that he spent three years as a trader for the quantitative trading firm Jane Street Capital. He formed his own trading and liquidity provider, Alameda Research, in 2017. FTX has grown rapidly to become the sixth-largest crypto exchange by volume, with a valuation of $3.5 billion. His political tendencies are no secret; he donated $5.2 million to the campaign of Joe Biden in 2020. He's a big proponent of the decentralized finance boom and is not impressed with Ethereum, instead promoting his own preferred platform, Solana, which we touched on briefly earlier in this chapter. Solana is the home of Bankman-Fried's decentralized exchange Serum, which launched in August 2020 with its token bearing the same name. He is believed to have crashed the price of his predecessor's Yearn.finance in October 2020 by shorting it. Bankman-Fried is already so well known that he's called only by his initials, SBF, by many in the industry. In October 2020 he shook up the market when FTX began offering fractional stock offerings, tokenized versions of shares of huge firms like Apple, Amazon, Google, and Tesla. Part of Forbes' 30 Under 30 list for finance, he has since launched FTX's Coinbase IPO futures and continues toiling towards his ultimate ambition—more than 1 billion people using defi and crypto.

3. **Michael Saylor:** The 56-year-old Saylor is the founder, chairman, and CEO of MicroStrategy, a business intelligence firm that he founded way back in 1989. Before getting into crypto, Saylor pretty much did it all including multiple degrees earned from MIT and a pilot in the US Air Force Reserve. In 2013, he bashed Bitcoin as a fad, and a quickly passing one at that. In 2020 he switched his viewpoint 180 degrees, as so many before and after him have done, and was quoted as saying, "Bitcoin, if it's not a hundred times better than golf, it's a million times better than gold, and there is nothing close to it." In August 2020, MicroStrategy

publicly announced it was buying $250 million of bitcoin for its treasury reserves. It bought $175 million shortly thereafter, then another $650 million in December for a total investment of $975 million in just three months. He has called Bitcoin a hedge against inflation which he feels is inevitable due to the country's difficulty with economic spending as a result of the pandemic. As of this publication, MicroStrategy held 70,470 BTC. Saylor is continuing to advise his investors to spend big on Bitcoin whenever possible and is starting to hold classes for corporations on the subject in 2021.

4. **Barry Silbert:** Silbert is the founder and CEO of Digital Currency Group, who is an early investor in the rypto industry, with his first transactions occurring all the way back in 2012, basically the foundational days at this point in time. This finance graduate of Emory University was working as an investment banker at Houlihan Lokey and was the CEO of Restricted Stock Partners back then. He was ahead of his time in forming Grayscale Investments and Digital Currency Group (DCG). Grayscale is most famous for its Bitcoin investment trust, while DCG allowed investors to plant seed money in blockchain-centered companies. Silbert was a famous early investor in both Coinbase and Ripple and has previously been named Ernst & Young's Entrepreneur of the Year. During 2020, DCG expanded into the cryptocurrency mining industry with a new subsidiary called Foundry that has the purpose of offering crypto mining equipment, financing for said mining, the mining itself, staking, and advisory services. It also will help out with the institutional demand for access to capital. As Bitcoin's price began to grow higher and higher at the tail end of 2020, Silbert bought a 30-second TV ad that appeared on major TV networks throughout the United States, urging viewers to drop gold in favor of crypto. It was a targeted appeal to older Americans who watch regular TV instead of streaming services and who are much more likely to still have a lot of their investment money tied up in gold instead of branching out to digital assets. A month after founding Foundry, DCG acquired the crypto exchange Luno,

which had provided the exchange seed funding back in 2014. At the end of 2020, Grayscale announced it had purchased about 3 times as much bitcoin as was mined in the final month of the year, and now had some $20 billion of bitcoin under its management for investors. In early 2021, Silbert stepped down as CEO of Grayscale for the purpose of concentrating on his role at DCG after its giant surge in growth during 2020. Silbert is contemplating turning DCG public, with commentators speculating such an IPO could command as much as $4 billion in investments.

5. **Hayden Adams:** The founder of Uniswap, Adams cut his teeth as a coder using the Solidity language that he learned on the Ethereum network. He calls getting laid off by tech powerhouse Siemens, "The best thing that ever happened to me." With the increase in free time, he started learning more and more about decentralized exchanges and automated market makers, allowing him to launch Uniswap for the first time near the end of 2018. It became a white-hot crypto project in 2020, riding the crest of the DeFi wave and is the biggest DEX—decentralized exchange—in terms of volume, even though its community came together to make a decision to shut down its UNI token. By November 2020, Uniswap had surpassed Coinbase Pro in daily exchange volume. The only thing negative to affect the company came near the end of 2020, when a coded copycat exchange calling itself Sushi Swap emerged and was able to pull liquidity from Uniswap, ultimately poising itself to become a competitor. A third version of Uniswap is coming in 2021 as the platform looks for improvements in the areas of scaling, governance, and automated money-making. While Sushi Swap's cone is perturbing, it is also forcing Uniswap to get better and leaner, which will ultimately increase its power.

6. **Juan Benet:** The 33-year-old Benet is nothing short of the American dream come to life. He was born in 1988 in Cuernavaca, Mexico, a city of 330,000 people about 90 miles from Mexico City but immigrated to the United States and wound up at Stanford

University where he ultimately earned an MS in Computer Science. He initially served as CTO of Loki Studios, running development on the multiplayer mobile game Geomon, which was acquired by Yahoo in 2013, making Benet and his fellow C-suite executives considerably richer in the process. He used his earnings to found Protocol Labs in 2014, using the Y-Combinator to start working on a number of projects, including Filecoin, the open-source, public cryptocurrency and digital payment system built on top of the InterPlanetary File System. Launched in 2017, it raised more than $200 million within 30 minutes of its initial coin offering. Users have the ability to rent out their own hard-drive space to log transactions on a blockchain. In 2020, three years after filing its ICO, the FIL token was listed for the first time on major exchanges, grabbing 118% in the first week of trading. Its storage topped 1 billion GB in November 2020, with Filecoin announcing a collaboration with Huobi that would fund a $10 million incubation center to support future endeavors. It wasn't all sunshine and rainbows for Benet, however. He got into a nasty Twitter battle with Justin Sun, founder of Tron, about the similarities between IPFS and Tron's BitTorrent File System that played out publicly and didn't show a good look for either man. In 2021, Benet expressed interest in improving the efficiency of how transactions use gas, especially in the light of distinct, consistent criticism about how so much power usage affects the environment. He's also exploring how encrypted transactions could be added to the environment to offer more security and break down the barriers that are still keeping so many people from joining the crypto revolution.

7. **Caitlin Long:** If you're from Wyoming and love cryptocurrency, Caitlin Long's name is the closest thing to a rock star you'll encounter today. Born in Laramie, Wyoming, she is a Wall Street veteran and holds a law degree from Harvard Law School. Like others on this list, she found out about and got hooked on Bitcoin early in the process—2012 in fact, and really locked on in 2013 when an article on how to buy and store Bitcoin came to her email

address. She was already passionate about making security markets fairer and working with honest ledgers, and that led her to cofound the Wyoming Blockchain Coalition in 2017, and served as the Chairwoman and President of blockchain startup Symbiont up through 2018. From 2017-2019, she was appointed by the governor of Wyoming to head the state's blockchain task force, is the chair of the state's nonprofit hackathon called WyoHackathon, and is the CEO of the Avanti Financial Group. Her insight and leadership helped Wyoming pass its 13 crypto/blockchain friendly laws expounded on in the previous chapter that turned the state into the most crypto/blockchain coveted location in the entire country. Her voice is a strong, clear one in the crypto regulatory arena, possibly the most important subject right now in the industry, where there is so much confusion, and the US government seems to have 10 different agencies with 10 different opinions on how crypto should be taxed, defined, and organized. In October 2020, she announced the founding of the first crypto-native bank in the US, Avanti Financial Group. The Wyoming State Banking Board gave it a charter to operate in Wyoming, alongside the San Francisco-based crypto exchange called Kraken. Long even advocated for JPMorgan Chase to move to Wyoming to avoid the tax crush it will endure from the fast-rising price of Bitcoin. Even with the pandemic shutting down most in-person events in 2020, Long has remained an active speaker, preaching to crypto companies to give as much transparency to the market as they can to avoid the mistakes of the traditional financial industry which led to people not trusting big banks. With the coming to office in 2021 of pro-crypto Republican Senator Cynthia Lummis, also a native of Wyoming, Long will likely be able to exert even more power on the country's handling of crypto, stating she hopes the politician can defend Bitcoin from government meddling and solidify the status of digital assets. The Wyoming Hackathon will triumphantly return in September 2021 and Long already has a heavy speaking schedule on her plate again.

8. **Vitalik Buterin:** We've talked about Buterin earlier in this book,

but no list would be complete without the 25-year-old whiz kid who has firmly entrenched Ethereum as the No. 2 crypto in the world with many prominent investors thinking it has the chops to be in the No. 1 position at the end of the day. Ethereum 2.0 is coming, and the world is already clamoring for it. If his energy-efficient proof-of-stake model can replace the current high-gas cost proof-of-work consensus model, Ethereum's costs are going to come way down and its usability and interest level should fly way up. ETH 2.0 is in Phase 0 at the time of this publication, which means there are people actually testing it now and it's gotten outside of Frankenstein's laboratory, a very positive sign.

9. **Mu Changchun:** The head of the People's Bank of China Digital Currency Research Institute is a powerful man just by way of that title and the fact that he has the position in a country of some 1.3 billion people. As China gets closer and closer to launching the world's first central bank digital currency, Mu is at the forefront of China President Xi Jinping's plan to outpace the United States to become the world leader in blockchain. Is that a bad thing? It certainly should not be. US and UK corporations have been noticeably slow to upgrade to blockchain technology despite all the benefits that have been shown on a smaller scale, particularly in environments like academia and healthcare. If China suddenly gears up with working, impressive blockchain technology and starts installing it to clients all over the world, the Western powers will be pitted with the choice of either letting China run wild with this economic windfall or powering their own serious bids to match it. The fact that Xi has unlimited power in China makes the country's bid to make the central digital currency a reality much faster than any other country could dare hope to match. Mu is planning to release a digital yuan with the bonus feature of 'controllable anonymity' that could be used to weaken the US's geopolitical influence and dramatically increase the shift away from paper banknotes.

10. **Gary Gensler:** Nominated for Chairman of the SEC as this

publication went to press, Gensler isn't some Johnny come lately to the crypto game but a professor who was previously teaching blockchain and digital assets at the illustrious American think tank MIT. For the first time in the short history of crypto being looked at by the US government, a face that actually knows about crypto and is clearly a believer in its potential is going to be spearheading the organization that has fought so hard to slow the currency's advancement at seemingly every turn for the last decade. Previous SEC chairman Jay Clayton made no secret about his skeptic attitude toward Bitcoin and its brethren, to the point where you had to wonder if all his confusing regulatory guidance and contradicting definitions of how crypto holdings should be defined and taxed were a long-term ploy to simply stall their advancement. Clayton's threatening of Ripple was among his most egregious slaps in the face, casting himself as the standard-bearer for what most crypto enthusiasts believe is the industry's biggest problem—not acceptance by the masses, but fear from those already established in the currency business; fear of competition and perhaps ultimately one day, becoming obsolete. Gensler, almost by default, knows more about crypto and blockchain than anyone else in the US government. He'll no doubt encounter roadblocks and stalling techniques along the way once he is approved to join President Joe Biden's new government, but one way or another a new, clear group of guidelines on regulating crypto and clearly defining what is and isn't a security is tangibly on the horizon. If Gensler gets his way, as many are hoping he does, approval for Bitcoin ETFs could not be that far behind. That's not to say Gensler will be a blind cheerleader for crypto, it still has its problems and its sore spots, but having a true expert in a position of leadership for the first time is a very exciting turn of events.

11. **Changpeng "CZ" Zao:** As the CEO of Binance, CZ has shown that he's not in the mood to sit still and let others do the heavy lifting for him. Running the world's largest cryptocurrency exchange might be enough of a day job for most executives but

being complacent has never been CZ's MO (pun intended). He's shown that aggressiveness in spades over the past year, introducing the Binance Smart Chain, the company's smart-contract as well as its own crypto token—Binance Coin (BNB), which by May 2021 had already risen to the fifth-largest cryptocurrency by market capitalization, humming along near the $35 billion mark. Perhaps the ballsiest move from CZ, however, was Binance's decision to pull out of the US in November 2020, kicking American clients to the curb and showing that crypto doesn't need to have a home in America when the American government seems bound and determined to trip it up and tax it at every turn. Every big name is bound to have some controversy attached to it, and CZ has his, attempting to sue two journalists writing for Forbes for publishing a story questioning his claim that Binance was no longer in control of Binance.US.

12. **Brad Garlinghouse:** The CEO of Ripple took the SEC's biggest punch and managed to keep standing when XRP was tossed from most US exchanges and lost its deal with MoneyGram. Garlinghouse says it's business as usual however, with more than a dozen new clients linked to its international payments, bank-centric network. However, more troubled waters seem on the horizon or perhaps already here considering the SEC filed a lawsuit against Ripple in the final 10 days of 2020, declaring that XRP is an unregistered security that has been selling illegally for seven years. As such, the SEC wants the staggering $1.38 billion that Ripple earned in crypto sales from that timeframe, a sum that —not surprisingly—the company does not have just laying around somewhere. It also wants Garlinghouse and Ripple executive chairman Chris Larsen to fork over the $600 million they made from said sales. Those back-to-back headshots led to Moneygram freezing XRP trading, a move that led to a precipitous drop in XRP's price. Its price per share fell 125% between December 17 and December 24, and dropped even further at the beginning of 2021. It's now regained its original value and actually closed above $1 a few times during May 2021,

but it had dropped to 7th among cryptos in a market where being outside the top two is a pretty steep drop.

13. **Brian Armstrong:** When you are head of a crypto firm, Coinbase that is going to have a potential $100 billion IPO, you tend to make waves. It doesn't hurt when your former general counsel is now acting Comptroller of the Currency and is making changes that finally give your industry some regulatory due, such as allowing banks to make payments with stablecoins. All that hype has been tempered by a not-so-smart move by Armstrong for having the worst response—none—to the Black Lives Matter movement, which saw 60 of its staff members quit in a combination of protest and solidarity. A pair of hit pieces from the New York Times suggesting Coinbase discriminated against both black and female employees had Armstrong going on the offensive, but even if he's proven correct, the damage is largely done.

14. **Dan Schulman:** Nobody has more respect for electronic currency than the CEO of PayPal, which has been doing the thing for a couple of decades now. However, Schulman has done a complete 180-degree turn on his crypto opinion in the past two years that you have to think has a lot to do with the staying power and skyrocketing value of Bitcoin. As recently as 2019 he was quoted as calling crypto a "reward mechanism" rather than a currency and that he wasn't seeing much appeal among his retailers for accepting digital assets for payment. In earlier incarnations of the industry, such a statement might have been a death knell, but two years later PayPal and Schulman have both done an about face. The company is launching a crypto service in the US, with rapid expansion plans for international markets. Some 29 million merchants are going to have to chase to accept payments in ether, litecoin, bitcoin, and bitcoin cash as a start. PayPal was a frontiersman in the initial push away from cash, and the corporation is apparently buying up a ton of bitcoin, with Schulman intimating that crypto is going to become a major part

of PayPal. In February 2021, he told Modern Consensus, "These initial steps are just the beginning of an extensive road map around crypto, blockchain, and digital currencies. We are significantly investing in our new crypto, blockchain, and digital currencies business unit in order to help shape this more inclusive future."

15. **Mike Novogratz:** When you start a company called Galaxy Digital, you're clearly expecting big things. It's been four years since Novogratz, a former partner at Goldman Sachs in the 1990s, launched the company that calls itself the "bridge between the crypto and institutional worlds." With business units in trading, investing, advisory services, and asset management, Galaxy Digital has grown to $1.2 billion in managed assets. Novogratz isn't fooling around when it comes to bold predictions, either. This year alone he's launched an Ethereum fund, blasted the potential of Dogecoin, and predicted Bitcoin will hit $100,000 before too long.

16. **Cynthia Lummis:** The crypto-friendly freshman senator from Wyoming—you've heard that name before—is a well-known Bitcoin owner as well as the mother-in-law of Unchained Capital's ace Will Cole. She's not just appealing to her fellow legislatures, but has taken to the airways, promoting crypto on podcasts around the country to go after the sensible, traditionalist crowd that seems to fear the unknowns of crypto the most. In February 2021, she hit the ground running by forming the Financial Innovation Caucus designed to educate not only senators but also their staffs on Bitcoin, blockchain, and everything else she can think of.

17. **Naval Ravikant:** Most well-known for his role as CEO of AngelList, which foments relationships between startups, job seekers, and investors, he fired up Metastable Capital recently, a crypto hedge fund. He doubled down with Spearhead Investment, which raised $100 million for its fund. It's hard to deny Ravikant

knows a winner when he sees one, he was one of the earliest prominent investors in both Twitter and Uber.

18. **Jesse Powell:** The CEO of Kraken is considering taking the exchange public and thinks the company can secure a $10 billion valuation. He's even more bullish on Bitcoin, believing the price could get so high that measuring it in dollars would be meritless. Despite its recent dip, he thinks it could hit $1 million in the next 10 years.

19. **Tyler and Cameron Winklevoss:** It takes a while to remember that these guys are not just fictional characters from "The Social Network" played so brilliantly by Armie Hammer a decade ago, and are in fact real investors who have had marked success, despite most everyday Americans knowing them mainly for their lawsuit against Mark Zuckerberg over the true nature of Facebook. The twin brothers have been on the crypto express for years, with Cameron called BTC "gold 2.0" in a well-read blog last summer. A new film is going to center around them based on the novel "Bitcoin Billionaires: A True Story of Genius, Betrayal, and Redemption." It's written by Ben Mezrich, whose first work was "Bringing Down the House: The Inside Story of Six MIT Students Who Took Vegas for Millions" and became the movie "21", and who more famously wrote "The Accidental Billionaires: The Founding of Facebook, A Tale of Sex, Money, Genius and betrayal", which became "The Social Network." The Winklevoss twins are widely acknowledged as the first people to become billionaires because of Bitcoin.

20. **Elon Musk:** No list of cryptocurrency movers and shakers is complete without Musk, who might not have the inherent power of China's president, but who is so pivotal to the rest of the world's crypto opinions that it's more than a little troublesome how much his every move, tweet, and action has on the price of multiple cryptocurrencies. Few don't know the name Elon Musk, but a deep dive into his personal and business history is worth

including in this book to understand how he got so powerful so quickly and became the face of crypto for many people around the world. Born in South Africa, he immigrated to Canada at age 17 to attend Queen's University, then jumped to Penn two years later where he selected a double major of economics and physics and earned both degrees simultaneously. Wanting to have his finger in a whole lot of different soups came naturally to Musk; his father has been an electromechanical engineer, pilot, sailor, property developer, and consultant throughout his life. He got interested in computers at age 10 in 1981 with his family's Commodore VIC-20 and taught himself how to program computers during the next two years using a manual. At age 12, he sold his original code of a video game designed in the early language BASIC to a magazine called PC and Office Technology for $500. Computers became his safe haven as he was very introverted and had been bullied at school; once thrown down a flight of stairs by boys with injuries resulting in his hospitalization. Moving to Canada might have been the best thing Musk ever did, as he was supposed to stay with his great uncle in Montreal, but couldn't locate him and packed a youth hostel instead. He did encounter a second cousin who took him west to live in Saskatchewan, and from there Musk worked odd jobs at a lumber mill and a farm, getting him out of his shell. In the mid 1990s he made his way to Silicon Valley for the first time, holding a pair of internships simultaneously—one with Pinnacle Research Institute, an energy startup, the other with Rocket Science Games. A year later he was accepted into Stanford's PhD program for materials science. He went through exactly two days of classes before dropping out, intent on joining the amazing Internet startup boom that was ongoing. As a wonderful piece of trivia for what was to come, Musk applied for a job at Netscape, but never got a response just before making the decision to go into business for himself. That same year, Musk, his younger brother Kimbal, and Greg Kouri combined to found the web software company Zip2 with funds from angel investors who helped the trio rent an office in Palo Alto, California. Everything he had went into that first business;

with no money beyond what the investors had offered, Musk slept on the couch of the office, showered at the local YMCA, and shared a single computer with his brother. He recalls sleeping during the day and coding all night on the group's first project, an Internet city guide that included map, directions, and yellow page listings that it marketed to big newspapers that were just getting their feet wet online. Within a few years, Zip2 had contracts with The New York Times and the Chicago Tribune. In 1999, at the ripe old age of 28, Musk and his fellow investors agreed to sell Zip2 to Compaq for $307 million in cash. Less than five years after dropping out of Harvard, Musk received $22 million in cash for his stake in the company; enough money for most people to live comfortably for the rest of their lives, but just the jumping-off point for his big brain. That same year, Musk co-founded X.com, which was a combination of online financial services and email payments. It was one of the first online banks to be federally insured, and the public took notice, with more than 200,000 users signing up in the first few months. The company got so big so quickly that investors became fearful of Musk's lack of experience and had him replaced as CEO. The following year, X.com merged with Confinity to eliminate the competition and Musk briefly returned as CEO. It also had a burgeoning payment system known as PayPal, which replaced X.com in the merger because of its established popularity. Musk returned as CEO but only for a time. He and PayPal's founder Peter Thiel, beginning his rise to Internet investor legend status, clashed over whether to use Microsoft or Linux for the company's technology, and Thiel resigned in protest. Musk continued to appear in over his head despite his original brilliant idea. The company struggled with tech and with the lack of a business plan, and for the second time in two years, he was booted as CEO, replaced by Thiel. The company was renamed PayPal with Thiel at the head, and a year later was acquired by eBay for a staggering $1.5 billion in stock. Musk, the largest shareholder in the company at 11.7%, received holdings worth about $175 million. As his portfolio grew, Musk turned his interest upward, quite literally, founding SpaceX in

May 2002, committed to privatizing space travel in his lifetime. SpaceX's first successful launch came six years later after three failed attempts, and all the investment paid off when the company received a contract worth $1.6 billion to send 12 flights to the International Space Station for resupplying runs. The company has since used an automated drone to dock with the ISS and become the first company to launch a manned rocket out of Earth's atmosphere to dock with the space station. In 2004, Musk first invested in Tesla Motors, joining its board of directors, and taking an active role in the company, overseeing the Roadster production design. He assumed leadership of the company as CEO and product architect in 2008 and built the world's first electric sports car that same year using lithium-ion batteries. As of March 2020, Tesla was the best-selling electric car in the world with more than 500,000 units sold and four different models. It had its IPO in 2010 and became the most valuable car maker in the world in the summer of 2020. Controversy reared its head for Musk at Tesla by the SEC in 2018 when he was sued by the commission for claiming funds had been secure to take the company private, which the SEC found to be misleading, false, and damaging to investors. He was fined $20 million and forced to step down as Tesla chairman for three years while remaining the firm's CEO. In 2006, Musk funded capital and provided the concept for SolarCity, which he acquired via Tesla in 2016. He first joined the Forbes Billionaires List in 2012 at $2 billion and in January 2021, briefly passed Amazon creator Jeff Bezos as the richest man in the world. When it comes to cryptocurrency, Musk took his time warming up to it. His first known interview on the subject came in 2014 when he was asked about it at Vanity Fair's New Establishment Summit and replied that Bitcoin was "probably a good thing, but primarily a means of doing illegal transactions." In 2017 as BTC moved past $8,000 and headed towards $20,000, an article appeared on Medium by author Sahil Gupta with the headline "Elon Musk Probably Invented Bitcoin". Gupta used a lot of circumstantial evidence that added up nicely for lots of sleuths and conspiracy theorists, even though Musk repeatedly denied it. Public opinion was onboard however, which led to a group of hackers using it to their advantage, stealing the credentials for two verified accounts on Twitter, changing those accounts names and pictures to pretend to be Musk, and enacting a fake cryptocurrency giveaway. Using Musk's likeness, the hackers stole $157,000 of victims' crypto before they were stopped by Twitter. In 2018, Musk finally began coming around on crypto, and in 2019 on a podcast with Ark Invest, he hailed Bitcoin as "quite brilliant" and added that "there's some merit to Ethereum." On April 2, 2019, Musk tweeted about Dogecoin (DOGE) for the first time, calling it his favorite cryptocurrency and pretty cool. In three days, the new crypto doubled in value, although that was only to a 'high' of $0.004. He moved the needle again in December 2020. On February 2, 2021, he simply tweeted the word "Doge" and the price rose 120% in four days. On February 8, 2021, Tesla bought $1.5 billion in bitcoin and announced plans to accept cryptocurrency as payment for its products. The day of the announcement, BTC closed at $9,876.75. It closed the next day at $10,129.44, a 2.5% jump. As Musk continued to tweet and talk about the future of crypto, and the rise of the COVID-19 pandemic saw millions begin to doubt the stability of the traditional financial system, BTC spiked in price to just shy of $64,000 on April 16, 2021. That's when the other shoe dropped and Musk as the leading face of crypto investing suddenly became tarnished. In May 2021, he announced via Twitter that Tesla would not accept BTC anymore as a payment method due its concerns over environmentalism and energy consumption of mining and confirming BTC transactions. The tweet caused a massive sell rush on the cryptocurrency that saw its price plummet from that April 16 high down to a May 24 opening price of $34,700.36, an 84% drop in value. As one observer noted, "If Elon Musk can decide the price of Bitcoin, it has failed as a currency." That statement is the growing concern of many observers and investors in crypto. The entire theory of crypto is based on the idea that no one entity—even something as powerful as the EU, the US, or China—can make the price go up and down. It is supposed to be beyond the whims of governments, corporations, and billionaires. Some have gone so far as to call Musk a problem for cryptocurrency, seeing as his tweets are moving multiple markets up and down. Imagine being a financial advisor and trying to sell a new customer on investing funds into a market where someone's tweets and words can jump prices at will. The foundational idea of Bitcoin in particular and crypto in general is that it is free of centralized control, and coming into the world after the disastrous effects of the 2008 financial crisis that brought on the Great Recession only served to reinforce that idea. Government does not control Bitcoin and cannot shut it down. His Bitcoin prowess is much more well documented, but Musk's seemingly playful attitude with the fate of Dogecoin is rather troubling. His tweets that pushed the price up were joined by the announcement he would host the American long-running comedy show "Saturday Night Live" on May 8, 2021. The price jumped 40% in the hours ahead of his appearance, on speculation that he would mention the young crypto to a national TV audience and the millions of people who stream and watch clips of the show later on YouTube. When he took center stage for his monologue that night in front of the live audience, he was watched live by 7.3 million viewers as well as 9 million viewers (to date) on YouTube. During that monologue, he introduced his mother to the audience and Maye Musk joked that she was looking forward to her Mother's Day present and hoped it wasn't Dogecoin—with Musk quipping that it was. Later the show's fake news broadcast, Weekend Update, Musk appeared as "Financial Expert Lloyd Ostertag" and hyped up Dogecoin, then performed an exchange with cast members Michael Che and Colin Jost on what Dogecoin actually is, eventually revealing that "it's a hustle." The coin's price dropped 30% after the joke was made. Not only is that sort of swing based on a lame joke made after midnight on a Saturday a little bit terrifying, it also makes it harder and harder to believe that governments and major financial institutes are ever going to risk their own assets into such a capricious investment. The scariest part of all might be that Musk isn't even trying to move the market one way or another, he's just being his normal, quirky self and the market is hanging on his every word and thought and lurching up or down accordingly. It's not just Internet conjecture that Musk is too powerful in crypto. At the CoinDesk Consensus 2021 conference, ARK Investment Management founder Cathie Wood leveled the blame for the Bitcoin drop on Musk saying it was "...exacerbated by Elon Musk, that there are some real environmental problems with the mining of bitcoin." Wood added that Musk probably got a few calls from other financial institutions after his move with Tesla away from crypto. Wood did hedge her comments by saying she feels Musk will b3.

Chapter 13
Cryptocurrency Around the World

We have focused a lot on how crypto is working in the US and China, but where are other countries in terms of usage and adoption? These updates are all the latest information as of May 2021.

Nigeria: Cryptocurrency is on the rise in this country of 201 million, with 33% of residents saying they are either using or own cryptocurrency. That's more than double the 14% of Americans who own crypto. In fact, Nigeria ranks first in the Statista Global Consumer Survey of 74 countries when it comes to enthusiasm for using or owning crypto. A big part of it is that Nigerians are increasingly focused on peer-to-peer phone payments as a large part of their economy. With Nigerians often sending money to or receiving money from family members in other countries, crypto offers a great alternative to the high price of transactional fees that come along with moving money across borders. In the past year, crypto plugins have become prevalent for phone payments, as Nigerians use them to send money to each other and to pay in stores.

Vietnam: Vietnam trails only Nigeria for usage by its population, with 21% involved at the time of publication. Kyber Network is the second-biggest user of crypto in the world, and the most successful startup in Vietnam's history with a $52 million effort in 2017. The link to crypto is the high number of adult gamers in the nation. 94% of the country's residents game on occasion and 20% game frequently, with this pastime changing the face of pro sports in the country. The two industries have been tied together by NFTs, RPG games, and the Internet of Things, used to buy upgrades to equipment in online games, clothes for avatars in games like Second Life, duels in games like Faraland, and so forth.

The Philippines: Remittance payments are a key role in the spread of crypto here. The country's Central Bank has approved of several crypto exchanges, giving them the right to operate as transfer and remittance companies. The Filipinio government is setting up a blockchain app with Unionbank to safely distribute government bonds. Unionbank also has a Bitcoin ATM in Manilla set up and running.

Peru: Peru has emerged as a somewhat surprising leader of crypto users in Latin America at 16% of its population. Brazil, Colombia, Argentina, Mexico and Chile, are also all in double digits. The upturn from Peru comes from presidential candidate Pedro Castillo, who has an interventionist policy in terms of economics and wants to nationalize things like oil, telecommunications, and mining in the country. Residents fear this policy will devalue the country's currency and are moving towards crypto as a reaction to guard against the possible plummeting drop in the value of their financial assets. If this happens, it will be following the trend of similar actions in Venezuela and Argentina where inflation has crushed those country's currency value, and crypto has been a viable investment alternative.

Turkey: About 20% of Turks are using crypto, but that number might be on its way down amid big news at the end of May 2021. Turkey has suffered problems with payments and with crypto exchanges failing, leaving investors high and dry. The country has added new rules to platforms making them part of the anti-money laundering (AML) and Combating the Financing of Terrorism (CFT) regulations that are global. All crypto service providers in Turkey must comply with these new regulations or be shut down. The government also announced it would establish a central custodian bank with the idea of eliminating counterparty risk. That will come as a welcome relief since earlier this year Turkey's central bank banned the use of crypto for payment. As soon as that ban was levied, two Turkish crypto exchanges, Vebitcoin and Thodex, both shut down trading, spurring fraud investigations. Thodex CEO Faruk Fatih Ozer has since fled the country, and is being tracked by both the Turkish government and Interpol, while six other people are in jail as a result of crypto fraud charges. Ozer was photographed fleeing the country with what authorities believe was $2 billion in investor assets. He made it through an airport security checkpoint ahead of authorities. The company's website shut down simultaneously. Ozer is thought to have fled to either Albania or Thailand. His actions left 390,000 users unable to access their digital wallets, with the thought that he has stolen funds from all of them.

Iran: The growing worry about the high cost in money and energy consumption caused by crypto mining has caused Iran to ban the practice for four months from June 2021. Iran President Hassan Rouhani addressed the media in that country in May because of major blackouts plaguing its cities. The country believes that crypto mining, which the country believes to be 85% illegal and unlicensed, is disrupting business and everyday life. The country has gone so far as to hire spies to begin a 'war' on unauthorized crypto mining and has authorities at every level on the lookout to prosecute illegal miners. Rouhani said that the authorized crypto mining in the country should not consume more than 300 MW of energy but that the unauthorized consumption is closer to 2,000 MW. Since the country's government is currently unable to distinguish between legal and illegal mining, it is instead banning everything. The capital city of Tehran has experienced daily outages, causing complaints, loss of revenue, and perhaps most dangerously making other countries perceive Iran as weak. According to a Bank of America report, rising prices for Bitcoin over the past two years have seen the carbon emissions caused by crypto mining to rise by more than 40 million tons. That's the equivalent of adding 8.9 million cars onto the highway systems in the same amount of time. Microsoft's Bill Gates has criticized Bitcoin mining as using more electricity per transaction than any other method in the entire world.

Chapter 14
The Future of Cryptocurrency and Blockchain

Considering how wild the first decade-plus has been for cryptocurrency and blockchain, it's hard to predict what the industry will look like next month, let alone 5, 10, or 20 years down the road. Consider the fact that at the time this book was started, Bitcoin was trading for $35,000 and as this sentence is written, the price is cresting above $58,000, a 66% increase in less than 60 days! That doesn't mean that experts, pundits, academics, and others haven't given it a go to take their best shots at what the future holds, however. Here's a look at what some of those thought leaders are projecting cryptocurrency's and blockchain futures to look like.

Deutsche Bank

Deutsche Bank views the current money system in place globally as fragile and believes that by the year 2030, there will be more than 200 million users of digital currency, this according to its Imagine 2030 report. That would still be only about 2.3% of the estimated world population of 8.5 billion at that point. The current era of fiat money—money based on trust, particularly that of a government to maintain the money's value—has existed since the early 1970s when the last major powers in the world disentangled themselves from the gold standard. Having fiat money in a political world has always been the financial equivalent of playing with fire in a room full of gasoline tanks—one bad move and everything goes up in flames. There are examples from all over the world—including many by global leaders otherwise thought of as conservative, morally-grounded people—of printing money or giving stimulus packages out to citizens for no reason other than political capital. Done too much, it devalues currency to the point where inflation makes it hard for many people to meet their basic needs.

While cryptocurrency has existed in reality for more than a decade, it only started to get real worldwide attention when Bitcoin surged to $20,000 in 2017. This past year, Facebook announced plans for its own cryptocurrency payment system Diem, formerly known as Libra, discussed earlier in this book—that could be the true game-changer, considering Facebook has more than 2 billion users worldwide, about 25% of the world's population.

The biggest hurdle for cryptocurrency to overcome is how to become a substitute, not just an addition, to the types of currency already in existence. It is a perplexing issue why that has not yet happened considering how many built-in advantages that crypto and blockchain technology possess, notably that they have great security at present, transactions move quickly, there are low transaction fees, and digital transactions in general are widely accepted by the overwhelming majority of the world's population. Other than the lack of a dollar sign, is there any objective difference in being paid 500 units of currency directly into your bank account, knowing that you can turn around and use 200 of those units to pay your rent, 100 to pay your bills, and 50 to buy your groceries? Regulatory hurdles remain the struggle for most cryptocurrencies, no matter how well-funded or thought out they are. A cashless society is already on its way, even if crypto had never come into existence.

If crypto is the payment of the future, one of the biggest things to overcome is to get India and China on board with its usage—neither government has shown much interest—and both have banned the sale and purchase of cryptocurrencies. By 2030, India will have surpassed China in population, and the two will combine for just shy of 3 billion people—about 36% of the entire world. In October 2020, the first ray of hope appeared in China when President Xi Jinping gave a ringing endorsement of blockchain as "an important breakthrough for independent innovation of core technologies." Both Xi and the People's Bank of China (PBoC) have made overtures about replacing cash with a digital currency issued by a central bank, but cryptocurrency is not anywhere in those plans. India will be a tougher nut to crack. While China's population is expected to grow by just 2% over the next 10 years, India's is increasing by 10%—in a nation already plagued by high levels of poverty, pollution, a weak infrastructure, gender inequality, and class inequality. Of course, those problems have existed in India for decades and have not kept the country from advancing its technology base, being aggressive in its space program, or developing nuclear weapons. How it deals with crypto is still anyone's guess.

If governments and regulators get onboard, the next step will be consumers and retailers. Will it be a fast switch or a slow one? Consider most retailers were very sluggish to accept digital payments, particularly on low-value items because they were paying fees themselves on transactions. If you're past a certain age you can remember a time when going to a convenience store and trying to buy a soft drink or a candy bar would get you hit with a large transaction fee by the salesclerk if your total came to less than $5. Digital payments are now preferred by most retailers because they eliminate several time-consuming and/or risky problems such as counting bills, making change, standing in line at the bank, and getting robbed. There are still lots of transaction fees, but they are fractional compared to previous decades. If cryptocurrency offers the option to remove those altogether or make them even drastically smaller, will retailers take the bait and make the switch? Deutsche Bank sees three big barriers keeping cryptocurrency from going mainstream, or at least be generally accepted. The first is legitimacy from the viewpoint of its two biggest critics—governments and regulators. The rise in the price of Bitcoin the last few years is very exciting if you're a proponent of crypto and blockchain, but the fact that it can rise and fall by tens of thousands of dollars per coin in a single day is not something that any legitimate government wants to get in bed with. Stability for pricing must be achieved somehow. A currency where one digital coin is worth $50,000 today, $75,000 tomorrow, and $25,000 in a week is nothing that consumers or merchants will sign off on. Additionally, there must be advantages for both merchants and consumers to using it. If I'm the average Joe consumer and I have $10,000 in the bank in dollars and $10,000 in my digital wallet in cryptocurrency, what is my advantage to buy my new smartphone in crypto as opposed to using my debit card? For that matter, why should the smartphone vendor bother accepting crypto when it already accepts every debit and credit card under the sun? A clear difference must be established, one that is not just obvious to entrepreneurs with long-term vision, but ones who are staying just above board on a month-by-month basis.

To get that sort of global reach takes a domino effort—where the biggest names in the market get onboard, which passes on intrinsic value to smaller players not only that this is a secure strategy, but one that they should feel compelled to join in for the purpose of staying ahead or at least on par with the competition and appealing to as wide a customer base as possible.

Vanquishing cash has lots of advantages, but also presents new challenges, particularly in the form of prolonged natural disasters and cyberattacks. In February 2021, a once-in-a-century winter storm hit the state of Texas in the US, overloading and freezing the state's electrical grid and knocking millions of residential and commercial consumers offline and keeping them without power for 72-96 hours. Wireless networks failed and people without any cash on hand had no way to purchase gas for their vehicles or food for their families. Hurricanes, earthquakes, tornadoes, and tsunamis can do similar types of damage.

Moreover, by freely admitting that everything financial is all digital, the target mark on banks and other financial institutions in the eyes of hackers and cybercriminals, not to mention terrorists, would balloon substantially. Taking down websites is already a mark of honor and a huge disruption; being able to cripple a country's entire financial system would be enough to get some black hat organizations positively salivating. Deutsche Bank holds the interesting and not unpopular opinion that the cryptocurrency, or stablecoin, that achieves a form of global acceptance has not been invented yet, and that major financial institutions and government powers on the level of the UN Security Council will be playing key roles in whatever is eventually adapted as a global virtual currency. That could spell bad news for all the major players of today, even mighty Bitcoin if they are not part of that process with their blockchain technology or cannot find some other avenue to stay relevant beyond as an investment vehicle.

Finyear

In its 2020 piece considering cryptocurrency as the potential future of money, Finyear presents an intriguing parallel between cryptocurrency as a technology and the Internet itself as a technology. The Internet is in some part of most people's day-to-day life in 2021, but most people barely knew what it was before the late 1990s. Before the creation of the web browser Mosaic, the Internet was almost exclusively used in academic settings and known as the World Wide Web. A quarter of a century later, it's gone from a passing fad to a source of entertainment to a fundamental component in an overwhelming number of businesses and as much a part of our culture as any invention that came before it. Could cryptocurrency see a similar rush to prominence in the next 10-15 years? Again, the hurdle of gaining acceptance by regulators looms, but beyond that is the one wave that always accompanies precipitous change: the power of youth. The Finyear piece mentions that about 18% of students in the US either own a digital currency or have done so in the past. These are individuals who are savvy enough to try something new and who are about 10-15 years away from being on the verge of becoming the country's policymakers and trendsetters. Their interaction with cryptocurrency today will chart the decisions they make tomorrow and going forward into the future. While fiat currency seems on the way out, the piece believes it may be the physical debit/credit card that vanishes first, particularly as smartphones and smartwatches continue to reach every corner of the globe. Already, apps like PayPal and Venmo are so well established that few people balk at accepting payment through one of them as opposed to a check or being paid in cash. Not only is it lightning quick, but the funds become immediately available in one's own account—no waiting for a check to clear or for a bank to hold a large cash deposit.

Cryptocurrency and Casinos

An absolutely natural fit for the present and future of cryptocurrencies is in the gambling industry, both in-person and online. Gambling is an industry that is legal in many states but still carries a degree of wanted anonymity and privacy from its users, which would allow a form of payment like cryptocurrency and a technology like blockchain to thrive. What are the advantages for casinos to use cryptocurrency? They include:

1. **No fees:** Casinos charge fees when converting your money to chips or credits; it's one of the ways they ensure they're making money off gamblers from the minute they log onto a site or walk into a casino. Using cryptocurrency would mean no conversions are necessary, the pay-in and pay-out system would not need conversions.

2. **No intermediary involvement:** No banks necessary for people to put funds into their online account. That means no banks peering

into a person's gambling spending when they are applying for a mortgage or a small-business loan.

3. **Increased personal safety:** Hit it big on a slot machine or at the craps table in Vegas and everyone around you knows about it, including the shady characters who might decide to keep tabs on you the rest of the night to see where you're staying, if you're alone, and plot a course to intercept you to relieve you of your wallet. If you're foolish enough to take your winnings in cash or back onto your credit or debit card, you're vulnerable. If your winnings go straight back into your cryptocurrency account, there's literally nothing to steal.

4. **Anonymity:** A big, big selling point for people who use websites and visit casinos, and value their privacy. Their reasons can be just about anything, but the fact remains the same.

5. **Data security:** Online gambling websites are ripe for the picking for hackers and cybercriminals. During 2019 and 2020, a team of Chinese hackers targeted gambling companies in Southeast Asia, Europe, and the Middle East, stealing company databases and source code while leaving the actual money untouched, which goes a long way towards not setting off alarms in those companies and can be more valuable in the long run for the thieves. Securing customers' data through blockchain can make it more difficult for criminals to get a hold of personal stuff.

Of course, there are plenty of negatives to the pairing of casinos and crypto, such as:

1. **Money laundering problems:** If you've ever seen a mobster movie or read any number of crime novels, you probably know that casinos are often a way for money laundering to take place—there are so many transactions and such a large cash flow that it's tough to pin down who's doing what. Someone who comes into $10,000 illegally can go to Las Vegas, turn it all into chips, gamble in small amounts for an hour or two, then cash back out

with a fresh set of bills. Rinse and repeat and you've got yourself a perfect setup. If it's that easy with fiat currency, imagine how easy it can be with a form of payment that doesn't even have a physical form and no physical currency changes hands. Since gambling winnings are not taxed in lots of jurisdictions, it makes it very difficult for government officials or tax authorities to monitor the transactions. Adding in the anonymity of blockchain technology would up that ante significantly. It's not just money laundering, either. That's a plenty serious crime, but that sort of operation can also be used for international crime organizations and terrorist funding. No casino wants to be involved in that line of work.

2. **Risk of a centralized network:** What happens at Caesar's Palace in Las Vegas means nothing to a casino in Atlantic City or Russia or the Middle East. They are all on different networks with their own security and their own way of doing things. But if every casino in the world was using the same form of cryptocurrency system, it would mean that any sort of data breach or hit on that system could take down everything at once, or make the cryptocurrency a huge target for online theft. Even the might of blockchain is not hacker-proof, as has been proven time and again in the past decade. The lock-and-key system and the cryptography might be failsafe on paper, but introducing the human aspect into anything brings risks with it. Factor in the idea that there are professional criminals who spend just as many hours figuring out how to hack a system as there are security experts working to protect it, and the risks mount.

3. **Lack of player acceptance.** The most delicate of the negatives is the fact that there are legions of gamblers around the world who have no idea what cryptocurrency is and no interest in learning about it or trying it out. It's understandable—if you're set in your ways and want your money in cash or in your classic bank account, what's the hook to change your mind? Obviously, at some point the world population will age to where the vast majority of gamblers are people who grew up in the age of the

Internet, digital financial transactions, and yes, even cryptocurrency, but that fixed point is a long way off for now. Again, it's about incentivizing. What does cryptocurrency offer to a gambler who has been playing quarter slots or the same two hour of blackjack at a specific table at the local casino for the past 10 years? What does cryptocurrency mean to someone playing in Indonesia or Nigeria or Brazil? If their favorite casino or website doesn't pay out or accept that cryptocurrency, it's utterly worthless.

IBM's Future of Blockchain

IBM is a company that has dove full force into the world of blockchain and is one of the industry's leaders in terms of practical solutions for modern problems. It has an online publication known as Blockchain Pulse that features regular blogs on all things blockchain, including one from April 2020 on the industry's potential future, addressing five key predictions, including:

1. **Emerging Governance Models:** Blockchain as it appears in the Bitcoin model is a dream scenario because it involves everyone and takes considerable precautions to ensure every transaction is validated before it becomes part of the chain. But in real-world applications like medicine, banking, and smart contracts, that sort of "everybody shares" mentality is going to keep blockchain from ever being used in a widespread, long-term capacity. Governance models for blockchain will incorporate AI to take new control of things like decision-making, payment qualifications, and permissions. Putting these systems in place makes blockchain understandable and within reach of a larger set of companies who struggle with the concept of the proof-of-work model that Bitcoin possesses. According to one survey, most CTOs and CIOS, 68%, expect to see a model for interactions of this sort across multiple blockchain environments in the next three years or fewer. That is a major step forward in the evolution of the technology's use, but one that will be absolutely necessary. If every company has its own blockchain component, but none of them are capable of

simple interaction with each other, it will be the equivalent of stepping back in time 40 years to the 1980s when every company was designing its own back-end system for things like payroll and invoicing, but none of them could communicate with the like-minded system at other companies.

2. **Adjacent technology will solidify blockchain as a massive data source.** We all know blockchain's security premise can keep data safe, secure, and anonymous, but so can a really expensive wall safe. The technology exists to be more than just a layer of protection; now that it is gaining acceptance in key industries and regions around the world, it needs to start getting integrated with other technologies that can take advantage of all its features. Once data is moved and protected, it needs to be audited, parsed, and analyzed through algorithms to sharpen a company's decision-making process. This provides better insights that a company can use to improve itself across the board in future endeavors, giving its customers more satisfaction, its partners more confidence, and itself more success.

3. **Better validation tools to fight fraud.** Blockchain isn't perfect, and when companies and individuals think it can't be manipulated, hacked, or cracked, it is at its weakest. Blockchain being invulnerable to hacking is the worst digital technology myth since the one about iPhones and Macs being incapable of being infected by viruses. A 2021 report from Atlas VPN found that blockchains were hit with 122 attacks in 2020 in which cryptocurrency, that is now valued at around $3.8 billion, was stolen. There were three major targets among those attacks. The first group consisted of decentralized apps that were running on Ethereum's platform. There were 47 of these that combined to steal $437 million worth of crypton—nearly $10 million per attack. Cryptocurrency exchanges were hit 28 times and lost $300 million in worth, and blockchain wallets were breached 27 times with a staggering $3 billion in losses, about $112 million per wallet hack. Those numbers are horrifying to read if you're a business owner, a

CTO, or just about anyone with major investments in cryptocurrency at the moment. That's a lot of money down the drain for a system that is supposed to be foolproof, and it is difficult to envision any companies except the largest getting on board with that sort of technology. The Amazons and Apples and Googles of the world can afford to put their own security systems in place to make their blockchain tools very difficult to break into, but what about all the small-to-medium sized businesses (SMBs) that make up the overwhelming majority of companies in the US? Even if they have a sound budget for cybersecurity, is it going to be enough to dissuade hackers and cybercriminals from recognizing that if they are using blockchain, they likely have valuable information inside? The last decade plus has shown that hackers love feasting on startups and SMBs because they often have little-to-no security in their shoestring budgets but have plenty of great information to swipe—customer names, credit card numbers, personal records, etc. SMBs suddenly investing in blockchain technology would look like the recent college grad who spends his or her first paycheck to put a down payment on a new sports car, then parks it in front of his rundown apartment complex. The clever criminals are going to notice the disparity there and do something about it. We can't expect perfection out of any Internet-based system, but it needs to be able to at least hold its own.

4. **Interconnectivity will advance**: Getting to the point where interconnectivity between permissioned and non-permissioned blockchain networks are all connected and can operate without major modifications might be decades away, but it's something that business leaders are already pushing for and will continue to do before they are committed to blockchain. That means either a big player or two will have to dominate the market with a scalable, compatible, affordable product, or great swathes of industries will be breaking off into factions that only use one blockchain system and doing business with them means converting likewise to it.

5. **Central banks will expand their services to include both wholesale and retail central bank digital currencies.** It hasn't happened in the US yet, but there are nations in the Middle East, the Caribbean, and Asia that are already rolling out trials of these so called CBDCs. CBDCs are different from established forms of fiat money in that the hope is to use them in conjunction with blockchain to lower the costs of payment systems and increase their efficiency. China has put out its digital yuan and South Korea has a demo currently in its pilot phase, but there has been no large-scale deployment to date. Most countries are doing things their own way, so that would be another challenge to overcome—some sort of centralized digital token that could be spent across borders. Venezuela, one of the world's premiere petroleum producers outside of the Middle East, launched its CBDC—the petro—in 2018. Backed by the country's crude oil reserves, it seemed like a great fit for a company mired in a recession. Within a few hours of its launch, investors had plucked up some $735 million worth of it. With inflation at a terrifying high rate, the Venezuelan government assured its citizens that the digital currency would help reverse that trend. However, it oversold its new toy, with the petro not available on any major crypto exchanges to be bought and sold by wealthy foreign investors. When media members began digging into whether the country's oil reserves were actually backing the currency. Multiple reports found that petro was actually backed by a national oil company known as PDVSA that was in debt itself by a whopping $45 billion. The situation went from bad to worse when Venezuelan President Nicolas Maduro converted citizens' pension bonuses into petro to increase the value of the currency. This coincided with then-US President Donald Trump banning Americans from buying the petro and led to a complete failure of the experiment. According to Deutsche Bank there are about 20 other digital currency projects making moves around the world, led by China's yuan and the US' digital dollar, which is still in a very formative phase. While cryptocurrencies are being created in giant multiples all over the world every day of the year, CBDCs could have a distinct advantage in that they could bring high levels

of traceability and transparency if done right by trusted central banks. The two main differences between a CBDC and a cryptocurrency are who runs them and what the supply looks like. While Bitcoin has a very well-publicized ultimate limit of coins that can be produced and distributed, a CBDC would be able to have its limit changed by the banking authority and the government behind it to counter things like economic downturns as well as facilitating national interest rates. Bitcoin has no true owner except for the people who own the crypto and anyone can run the software without needing permission. Central entities for a CBDC would also dictate which financial organizations could participate in its management. In many ways, the CBDC push started when Facebook announced its Libra (now Diem) plans in 2019. Fearing the possibility of a company with more than 2 billion followers suddenly offering a cryptocurrency as an alternative to their own banking systems, countries turned to their central banks to come up with a viable solution to keep Facebook on its heels. While Mark Zuckerberg and the powers that be at Facebook might not agree, their announcement of a cryptocurrency, digital wallet, and smart contracts might have been the best thing to happen to cryptocurrency and blockchain as a whole because of the fear it spurred in other financial institutions around the world. The famous axiom that "change happens when the pain of staying the same is greater than the pain of change" definitely holds water for these banks now toying with CBDCs around the world. Most financial powers around the world scoffed at the very idea of cryptocurrency during its infancy and only began to take it seriously as Bitcoin began shattering price ceiling after price ceiling and more and more companies started trialing and succeeding using blockchain solutions like Ethereum for their pain points. Once the first big player—Facebook—jumped into the crypto market, suddenly it looked infinitely more appealing, or at least the fear of falling behind forever in the next phase of the financial evolution scared national banks into doing their own research and development and seeing what they can shake out. With Facebook still unable to put a target date on when its digital assets will be released, these countries have a window of opportunity to beat the social media giant to the punch.

Conclusion

In just over a decade, cryptocurrency has generated the biggest buzz of any financial and technological revolution in decades. While the markets for many of the actual currencies has seen extreme volatility as people struggle to incorporate what role each of these currencies and technologies will play in their lives, there is no doubting that the technology behind these companies is not just game-changing, but a provisional look at how many digital transactions will take place in the future. The ability to ensure that transactions are sealed airtight and cannot be changed, erased, or reversed, is a huge security sigh of relief and could have enormous value in arenas like medicine, personal finance, and more. More than 12 years since its revelation, blockchain remains a huge subject of study and fascination for companies and individuals alike, with its applications already taking shape in our society.

www.ingramcontent.com/pod-product-compliance
Lightning Source LLC
Chambersburg PA
CBHW081819200326
41597CB00023B/4314

REFERENCES

- Rothschuh KE, The conceptualization of hydrotherapy in the 19th century. J. H. Rausse, Theodor Hahn, Lorenz Gleich, Gesnerus. 1981;38(1-2):175-90. PMID: 7014376 [PubMed - indexed for MEDLINE]
- Kirchfeld, Friedhelm, and Wade Boyle. "Nature Doctors: Pioneers in Naturopathic Medicine". Medicina Biologica, 1994
- Kuhne, L., *Neo-Naturopathy: The New Science of Healing,* Lust Pub. Co., New Jersey 1917
- Schramm, A.C., *ISNP archives,* Los Angeles
- Collins, F.W., First National University archives
- Shelton, H., "What Have We, Nature Cure or a Bag of Tricks?" *Naturopath and Herald of Health,* (1921) 26:283-7
- Gehman, J.M., "To Honor the Father of Naturopathy", *Nature's Path* (1947) 51:19
- Holly J. Hough et al., Profile of a Profession: Naturopathic Practice, Center for the Health Professions, University of California, San Francisco, 2001
- *Herald of Health and Naturopath,* July 1947
- Spitler, H.R., Basic Naturopathy, American Naturopathic Association 1948
- Wendel, P., Standardized Naturopathy, Wendel, 1951
- Gehman, J.M., Official Bulletin of the American Naturopathic Association, Inc., Jan. 25, 1948, Washington, DC
- The American Association of Naturopathic Physicians, "AANP Definition of Naturopathic Medicine Position Paper", 2004
- Whorton, J.C., Nature Cures: The History of Alternative Medicine in America, Oxford University Press, 2002
- American Naturopathic Medical Association web site
- American Association of Naturopathic Physicians web site
- International Society of Naturopathic Physicians web site
- Department of Regulatory Agencies web site: http://www.dora.state.co.us/opr/archive/2008NaturopathicPhysiciansSunrise.pdf
- Barrett, Stephen (2003-06-13). "Naturopathic Accreditation Agency Loses Federal Recognition - But Reapproval Seems Likely". Quackwatch. http://www.quackwatch.org/01QuackeryRelatedTopics/Naturopathy/accreditation.html. Retrieved 2009-04-17.
- *Discover the Nature of Good Medicine: 2007-2008 Course Catalogue,* Southwest College of Naturopathic Medicine
- Department of Health, Education, and Welfare, "Independent Practitioners Under Medicare" report, section on naturopathic practitioners
- *Journal of the American Naturopathic Association,* October 1949
- *Journal of the American Naturopathic Association,* June 1949
- Fehr-Snyder, K. "Naturopathic board director on leave". Arizona Republic, May 11, 2001. Naturopathic Board votes to votes to fire chief: Allegations tied to credentials, paper shredding. Arizona Republic, May 12, 2001.
- Davenport, D.K. *Performance Audit: Arizona Naturopathic Physicians Board of Medical Examiners.* Report No. 00-9, June 2000.
- Minutes of the Idaho Board of Naturopathic Medical Examiners, Oct. 2007
- *The Spokesman-Review,* "Naturopath Repeal Clears Committee", Jan. 27, 2009
- *Nature's Path,* Jan. 1928, p. 12
- *Nature's Path,* Mar. 1928, p. 105
- *Nature's Path,* Jul. 1928, p. 226
- *Nature's Path,* Jul. 1930, pp. 196-215
- *Nature's Path,* Dec. 1930, p. 359
- *Nature's Path,* Jan. 1931, p. 26
- *Nature's Path,* Apr. 1931, p. 104
- *Nature's Path,* Jun. 1931, p. 173
- *Nature's Path,* Jun. 1931, p. 183
- *Naturopath and Herald of Health,* Jan. 1937, p. 26
- *Naturopath and Herald of Health,* Mar. 1937, p. 90
- *Naturopath and Herald of Health,* Jun. 1937, p. 175
- *Naturopath and Herald of Health,* Jun. 1937, p. 163
- *Naturopath and Herald of Health,* Aug. 1937, p. 254
- *Naturopath and Herald of Health,* Dec. 1937
- *Journal of the American Naturopathic Association, Inc.,* Oct. 1949, p. 17
- *Journal of Naturopathic Medicine,* Sept. 1950, p. 20
- *Digest of Chiropractic Economics,* July/Aug 1978, p. 101
- *Textbook of Natural Medicine,* Vol. 3, Chap. 3, p. 37
- Grunwald, Jorg, PhD; The European Phytomedicines Market--Figures, Trends, Analyses; *HerbalGram* 34, Summer 1995

Botanical illustrations courtesy of www.openclipart.org. The images were donated by Pearson Scott Foresman, an educational publisher, to Wikimedia Commons, and are thereby in the Public Domain. Wooden doctor carving photo is © Sarah Klochars-Clauser for openphoto.net.

"Remember, that group of people are pseudo medical men and just as soon as they get power they are going to be no better."

--Otis G. Carroll, ND

www.ingramcontent.com/pod-product-compliance
Lightning Source LLC
Chambersburg PA
CBHW081818200326
41597CB00023B/4300